Just F*cking Do It

Just F*cking Do It

Stop Playing Small. Transform your life.

NOOR HIBBERT

First published in Great Britain in 2019 by John Murray Learning, an imprint of John Murray Press. An Hachette UK company.

A CIP catalogue record for this title is available from the British Library

Paperback: 978 1 473 69275 6
eBook: 978 1 473 69296 1

Typeset by Cenveo® Publisher Services.
Printed and bound in Great Britain by Clays Ltd, Elcograf S.p.A

John Murray Learning policy is to use papers that are natural, renewable and recyclable products and made from wood grown in sustainable forests. The logging and manufacturing processes are expected to conform to the environmental regulations of the country of origin.

John Murray Learning
Carmelite House
50 Victoria Embankment
London EC4Y 0DZ
www.hodder.co.uk

Dedication

Firstly, I dedicate this book to my three beautiful daughters Layla-Rose, Safia-Lily and Amira-Jasmine.

If there is anything in life that I wish for you girls, it's to dream bigger then you ever thought possible and to take relentless action towards making every dream a reality. You gave me my fire and I'm so grateful you chose me to be your mother. I love you unconditionally with every cell in my body.

I also dedicate this book to my incredible mother, who is the epitome and embodiment of the Just F*cking Do It mantra in every way. Thank you for your unwavering love and support and for showing me how to take relentless action towards achieving anything I want.

Acknowledgements

There are so many wonderful people who have helped me to make this book a reality.

My first heartfelt thank you goes to my husband and best friend Richard, who has continually supported me over the years. Thank you for putting up with all my crazy ideas, for helping me to believe in myself when I had doubts, and for being the best father to our girls which has enabled me to do my art and build my business. And for loving me and showing me that love can indeed be so real.

Thank you to my incredible father who has always been a source of support for me and my moral compass in life. I'm so grateful for all the learning in our relationship and for our growing together through the years. I have learned so much about myself through you and I thank you for allowing me to share my learning in this book.

To my amazing literary agent and friend Jessica Killingley of the BKS Agency. The Universe conspired to bring us together. No amount of words can describe the gratitude I have for your belief in me. Without you I don't know if this book would here now. And to James and Jason who are the other two-thirds of the agency and have shown me loving support in making this book a success.

To my lovely, kind and funny editor Jonathan who held the space for me to share my message with the world, in my own words. I always love coming to visit you. And to Nicola and the rest of the team at John Murray Learning for helping to bring it all together. You have all been a joy to work with.

Lastly, to all the incredible women who've been my clients over the past few years. I acknowledge all of you because you let me be part of your journeys and your stories. If it wasn't for you I'd have no business. I truly wish you all the success in the world.

Contents

About the Author

Photo: © Nabila Burija

Noor Hibbert is a qualified life and business coach, serial-entrepreneur, motivational speaker, author, mother and spiritual badass.

Noor has a degree in Psychology and a Postgraduate Certifications in Business & Executive Coaching and Coaching Psychology.

She is a Senior Practitioner certified by the European Coaching and Mentoring Council (EMCC).

She has created two six-figure businesses in just three years, whilst raising three small children and embarking on a spiritual journey which has accelerated her success.

She regularly travels around the globe, running events in the US and UK.

1

The Good, the Bad, the F-ugly

This is your one life: make it a 'fuck yes' type of life.

You have probably picked up this book because there is a voice inside you whispering that you are meant for more and because there's a part of you that wants to be happier. Like really fucking happy. If we whittled down why we all do the things we do in life, the underlying reason is that we want to be and feel happy. We want to have jobs we love so we can be happy, a partner in life to make us happy, have a body we love so we can look in the mirror and feel happy, and experience things in the world that bring us happiness. Happiness makes us feel good, and feeling good is the goal for most humans.

Most people I speak to who aren't feeling the level of happiness that I truly believe we all deserve feel that way because deep down they know they are destined for so much more. The thing is, I believe we were put on this planet to do extraordinary things, to be wildly abundant and to have all that we desire. We are all destined for a life living like a rock star in our own version of a Hollywood movie, where we are the star of the show. But somewhere between birth and adulthood, a lot of us got sold into a very different dream. If you're working in a job that bores you senseless, are broke and continuously have more month than money, have physical ailments that won't disappear, in a relationship that drains you emotionally or find yourself feeling like everything is a pointless waste of time, then let me tell you, my friend, you have bought into the wrong life and we need to change that – together.

All about me

So, who am I and why should you bother investing a few hours of your priceless time with me? I am a transformational mindset coach and my goal is to help people transform their lives personally and professionally so that they can become shamelessly happy by having it all. Yes, you can have it all. You can have a vocation that excites you, a relationship that fulfils you, a body that you feel amazing in and even the financial wealth you think is only for the 'other half'. You can have your cake and eat it and my mission is to help people become more conscious, stop living life on autopilot, and go out there, bake the tastiest goddamn cake and devour it, slice by slice.

I am also just a normal girl and mum to three pretty awesome human beings who in fact hugely spurred my decision to make changes in my life. I love hanging out in my gym gear (even when I am nowhere near a gym or have any intention of going to one that day), am a meditation junkie, eat vegan and love travelling. I went to university to study Psychology, and have a Postgraduate Certificate in Business & Executive Coaching and another in Coaching Psychology. I am obsessed with the inner workings of the human mind and the outer workings of our often crazy human behaviour.

I wrote this book with the intention of it being your wake-up call and to offer you a new perspective on how life can be limitless and wide open with possibility. I want to give you a chance to transform your thinking and to make you under-stand that, whatever situation you are in right now, you have the power at your fingertips to consciously change it on your own terms. This book is about helping you to do what you need to do to go for your dreams and finally get the stuff done that you have been dreaming about – the things that are ulti-mately going to make you feel ... yes ... happy.

That is why you bought this book – because either you know you are not living your full potential or because you look good on paper but inside you like feel like a fraud. Perhaps you are living a life that you know was not meant for you or you are not showing up as the 100 per cent authentic individual that you know you could be. Whatever the reason, you know that there is more out there, and you want to learn how to get it.

4

I want this book to be the hug of support you have been waiting for and the metaphorical kick up the booty so you can go for it. It's time to do whatever you need to do, to change *whatever* you need to change.

I get that there are truckloads of books out there on personal development – heck, I own a hell of a lot of them, but this book is different. My clients pay a lot of money to work with me directly, and I honestly know that's not accessible for everyone, so these pages are your chance to have me hold your hand and to get you the success you want for the cost of a couple of coffees, minus the calories. This book isn't just about theory; it's about practice. It's about habit-changing, booty-shaking, routine-making and digging deeper than you will ever feel comfortable about – but who said change was easy?

If we were to lay all the cards out on the table, I have massively taken one for the team for you in acquiring the evidence for this book! I have spent many, many hours of my life speaking with private coaches, have flown a ridiculous number of miles across the planet to attend seminars where I had to hug more strangers than has ever felt normal, and I've invested in more self-help audiobooks then my phone can handle, but I did it all in pursuit of the kind of change that I will share with you in this book. I solemnly promise to take you step by step through a mind-altering journey of self-discovery and personal transformation to help you be, do and have whatever you want. Can I hear an *amen*?

I know that what I will teach you is pretty impressive because I have been on that journey and still am. You may be wondering how a middle-class, Middle Eastern girl from an affluent part of London is qualified to talk about pain and happiness. After all, my siblings and I had a nice house, a private school education and parents both in good jobs. But internally my life felt very different.

Let me give you a little bit of background on my family and my childhood so that you can understand where I came from. My dad is Iraqi, religious and pretty traditional in terms of how we were brought up. He was very strict, had a terribly short fuse and desperately tried to shield us from the perils of the Western world, including sex, drugs and rock and roll. If he'd had his way, we wouldn't have watched 12-rated films until we were 18 and he would have banned 18-rated ones until we were dead. God forbid that we saw two humans kissing – that would have been the end of the world!

My dad worked incredibly long hours as a lawyer, found it uncomfortably hard to show any affection to us children and had a turbulent marriage with my mum. She was the total opposite to him in every way. She would sneak us out to a get non-halal McDonald's, let us secretly wear clothes my dad would have hated and let us watch films we weren't allowed when he wasn't around. She is an Iranian with a very Western attitude who called everyone and anyone 'Darling!' Even that pissed my dad off. This resulted in us living in a war zone as children and them eventually divorcing. I became estranged from my dad for many years after that and always felt the absence of a strong male role model in my life, though our relationship had been very fraught to begin with. I loved my dad but I just never understood him and the way he thought about how life should be.

It was at the age of four that I first realized I felt different – and it hurt. When I say different, I mean not totally white, and with a name that people could never pronounce. I was in the school playground, minding my own business, when a girl boldly walked up to me and asked me why my eyebrows were so bushy and why I was so ugly. Ouch! I didn't have an answer but spent the rest of the day inspecting all the other children's eyebrows in the school. Mine distinctly met in the middle and I realized in that moment that I was different. I went home, cried, blamed my parents and carried the burden of the bushy brow until I was 11, until the fated day I took a pair of tweezers and began what can only be described as an eyebrow massacre. Although thin eyebrows were in during the late 1990s, I looked horrific and my poor mother almost had a heart attack.

To add insult to brow injury, I spent most of my early teenage years getting bullied, feeling left out, and not knowing where I belonged. I wanted to change my hair colour, change my name, change my parents and just be 'ordinary'. There was an internal pain that I couldn't shift and by the age of 16 I was medicated on Prozac, drinking Malibu that I had stashed under my bed to make me feel normal and spending time trying to ever so gently self-harm (I didn't really like the pain all that much). So, let me tell you, I know what it's like to feel low, confused and to keep asking yourself on repeat 'Is life meant to be this hard?'

By the age of 20, I had already experienced the gut-wrenching pain of several heartbreaks, the angst that came with navigating the emotional minefield of my parents' divorce and then trying to settle into a university life that provided its own ups and downs. I had become well versed in the language of victimhood and my default state seemed to be set to 'dramatic'. I battled with fitting into my family, fitting in with friends, fitting in with life and finding relationships that didn't drive me crazy. When your expectation of what the world should look like is vastly different from what it is, you suffer from depression. When you continually battle with accepting who you are at the very core, you suffer from anxiety. When you don't know what your purpose is and can't accept yourself, it manifests in physical ailments. I was ashamed to be me because I wasn't popular, skinny or academically clever. I felt different and I *despised* being different. Why couldn't I just fit in?

To be honest, even after I got through some of my lowest points, I still spent most of my twenties confused as to what my purpose was and how to get my shit together so I could feel happy and become the heroine in my own Hollywood movie.

If you could scroll through my old Facebook photos right now, you would see a girl who spent most of her time drinking, drunk or hungover. A girl who sought solace in class A drugs and a girl who rebelled against everything she was brought up to believe was right. You would see a girl on a never-ending journey to find Mr Right and yet disastrously re-enacting *How to Lose a Guy in 10 Days* over and over again. (I love that film!)

So, let me tell you, I may be 'qualified' academically to help you out, but I have also exuberantly attended every stage of the (sometimes rather painful) school of life and got ripped-up T-shirts to prove every step. The first thing I want to tell you is, wherever you are today, right now, is not where you have to be next week or next month or next year. I figured out a secret that dramatically changed things for me. This secret has helped me go from earning £138 a week on maternity pay to making multiple six figures a year, giving me the freedom to travel when I want, put my children in the best schools, invest in properties and even enable my husband to retire from his job. It has helped me have the body that I had always dreamed of, a marriage that makes my heart sing and relationships with my children that flourish every day. It has also helped me to form the most authentic and loving relationships with my parents so that they are totally accepting of me, my choices and my lifestyle. I never thought I'd be able to say this when I was younger, but today my dad is one of my best friends and loyal supporters, and I can be totally me. Basically, I am now a jammy so and so.

But more than that, this secret has helped me to become happy. Not 'social media show' happy but *actually* happy. Like lying in bed with unabashed gratitude that I feel so damn happy kind of happy. I stopped worrying about what everyone wanted from me. I stopped wanting to please everyone and fit in. I stopped focusing on what everyone else had and what I didn't and started to create a life that was arguably, quite selfishly, all about me. And I have used that secret to help my clients across the world dramatically change their lives.

And now I am going to share it all with you in this book.

All about you

As a recovering depressive, anxiety-sufferer, life-plodder and self-confessed drama queen, I am in a unique position to show you that there is a way to transform your life, and I am going to help you take those steps. I know it's a big job, but I am willing to take it on because, if I can change my story, then so can you. You have the power. If you don't like your story, then it's bloody time you rewrote it. I also want to let you know that you don't need to wait until your life chokeslams the shit out of you and you are on the floor drowning in your own tears before making a change. Now is your time.

So, let me tell you my secret: changing your life starts with changing your mind. Maybe you have had heard this a gazillion times before and thought it was a load of hogwash, or perhaps you have never heard this until now. But whichever camp you're in, you need to listen to it (again).

But here is the caveat: *it isn't simple or easy changing your mind.* In fact, I would go as far as to say it is one of the hardest things for most humans to do, which is why we have ended up with a planet full of way too many people who feel stuck and even hopeless. From the moment we are born, we are thrust into a world where we have thoughts, ideas and experiences imposed upon us that lead us to form a set of beliefs about the world. Beliefs are essentially the guiding principles that provide direction and meaning in life. Beliefs are the pre-set filters to our perceptions of the world. Beliefs are like 'internal commands' to the brain as to how to represent what is happening, when we believe something to be true.

From childhood, we become like sponges that soak *everything* up – the great, the good, the bad and the really fucking ugly. If our parents are broke and worrying about money, we start to form beliefs about that. If our parents show us love and we come from fun and loving households, we will develop beliefs about that. If your parents argue all the time, you will form a view of your world because of that. We become conditioned to see the world in a certain way based on what our childhood experience was like. This all creates and determines our outlook on the world.

Our brains are made up of many parts, but there are two things we need to fully comprehend. We have a conscious mind and a subconscious mind, and for the most part, our subconscious mind runs the show, based on all the stuff that happens when we are kids, as explained above. This forms the template rooted in our brain that guides our thoughts and governs our actions as adults. From a psychological perspective, we need to change the template to make sure that it serves us in getting success and happiness in all areas of our lives. And changing our unconscious takes some work and can, quite frankly, be as painful as getting your privates waxed.

Most of us feel we have no control over our destiny because we are living by a template that has been manufactured by our parents, teachers, culture, government and media. At birth we are given the gift of a whole palette of beautiful colours enabling us to paint the most incredibly vibrant life. Yet, as each year passes, we become conditioned to believe that life is an endless chain of eat, sleep, work, repeat. Most of us end up believing that life is limited and restricted. Tragically, instead of believing that we are the powerful artists we are, and behaving accordingly, we become a victim of our own story. Every time we buy into a belief of fear and scarcity, we give away a colour from our palette and our potential to paint an incredible picture of what our life should be like is diminished. That's why so many people are not fulfilled, and life feels so … beige. In essence, we have forgotten who we truly are.

Most people I speak to sing the same tune. They feel unful-filled, as if they are failing and lost about what their path should be. For the most part, their life lacks passion, purpose and a sprinkling of va-va-voom because their paint palette now lacks the resources for them to paint a truly beautiful picture. Many of us buy into the story that making money is hard, that we should strive for a 'comfortable' life, that we should be grateful for what we have and not want more. We are sold into the idea that life is for working and that dreaming is for idiots. We believe that there is only so much love and success to go around so we had better whip out our boxing gloves and fight for it. We buy into self-sabotaging beliefs that say, 'Who am I to have it all?'

People work hard five out of seven days to be able to afford the material objects that they think will bring them happiness and that they believe represent success. Once they attain the object, they realize that it hasn't filled them up, so they get into debt trying to buy more things to fill the void just to wake up every morning and still feel unhappy ... and even more broke. The cycle goes on and on.

A great example of this are the countless celebrities who end up as alcoholics and drug addicts. I remember always think-ing 'How can they be depressed, they are loaded?!' As Russell Brand poignantly says in his book *Recovery: Freedom from Our Addictions*: 'We have been taught that freedom is the freedom to pursue our petty, trivial desires. Real freedom is freedom from our petty, trivial desires.' As I went on my journey of personal development, I realized that success and happiness are not just about the acquiring of money or material objects – it runs so much deeper than most of us care to explore in our busy mod-ern Western world.

In the spirit of making everything in this book super clear, I want to break down a few things and what I mean by them and why I feel they are crucial. I will give you definitions of what I mean when I 'speak psychology' so that you can grasp important concepts. I will explain those concepts and why they are relevant to you making changes in your life. I will illustrate my ideas with stories about people just like you, because I can guarantee one thing – there may be billions of people in the world, but our patterns of behaviour are almost always very predictable and the things that hold us back are virtually all the same. I will also be giving you 'Just Fucking Do It!' (JFDI!) exercises and practical actions so that you can consolidate what I am teaching you in order for you to actually get results. Finally, I want you to shamelessly *just fucking do it.*

To get us started, I want to give you a few examples of what non-serving conditioning looks like and the effect our childhood experiences can have on our future. Perhaps these will resonate with you.

LUCY'S STORY

Lucy grew up in a 'working-class' household where her parents both worked full time so had little quality time with their kids. They still struggled to make ends meet and argued a lot because of this. When Lucy had a family of her own, she was always fearful about not having enough money. She and her husband worked, and although they were better off financially than her parents, Lucy would argue with her husband about money. Lucy also never pushed herself to get a better job because she didn't see the point, as she thought it would involve even more hours away from her family. Lucy's 'templates' were sabotaging her potential to create a life of abundance for her family.

RICHARD'S STORY

Richard had come from a family of high-achieving academics and so followed in their footsteps to become a teacher. He worked his way up to become head teacher. His family was proud of him, but he didn't feel fulfilled. He had simply followed his parents' path. He then decided to quit and start his own business. Throughout his business, he felt uneasy that people were judging him as he was no longer in the teaching world.

He had a belief that he wasn't doing a 'proper job' even though he was making up to five times his previous salary. Richard's template was interfering with his success and happiness.

Examining these examples through the lens of psychology gives us immediate insights into the way we all behave; we respond to our experiences with responses formed under our unique circumstances. To understand why we respond the way we do, we can use psychological principles to shed light on our behaviour.

Those are just two examples, but you can already see that psychology is essential to understanding what is holding us back and making us unfulfilled and unhappy. It forms the basis for all the principles that I will share in this book – principles which will help you examine and rewrite that template which is an overriding factor in preventing you from reaching your full potential. It's like owning a gorgeous brand-new Ferrari. You sit in it knowing that it could take you on a wonderful journey but when you start the engine and rev it up, it doesn't move. You take it to the garage and the engineer informs you that it's been badly programmed.

You are that Ferrari. You have all the potential, beauty and power to go on any journey and yet you are struggling to move because of faulty programming. It's time to reprogram you, baby.

Your secret weapon

Let me be clear, this is not just another book on psychology and mindset because I have seen people read such books and yet still not feel as though they have the success in life they want. In fact, I was one of them. I had read some mindset books, created my first business, and was even earning great money. I was looking like a success on the outside – but something inside didn't feel right. I realized that, although improving your mindset is undeniably important, there is also another vital factor in transforming your life and achieving a rounded sense of success. And it is something that so many people fail to understand is their secret weapon, at their disposal at any given time.

I want to get something clear from the outset: success doesn't simply mean financial wealth. Nor is success ever defined in the same way for every person. Success for one person may be a loving relationship and for another a healthy, fit and toned body. My idea of an extraordinary life will be totally different from yours and yours totally different from another reader's. We will define what your own extraordinary life looks like shortly and you will have free rein to pull out a brand-new paint palette full of whichever colours you like and paint that picture however you want. You are not a robot. This is your life, and it's time to live it. You do not need to buy into the idea that you can only have success in one part of your life. To feel true happiness is to have success across all areas of your life, and that is exactly what I want for you – this secret weapon is here to help you.

In the interests of total transparency, when I first heard about this secret weapon, I didn't believe in it because, after years of having religion shoved down my throat, I had decided to become an atheist. But as my life has unfolded into something better than my dreams, I can now sincerely and wholeheartedly tell you this way of thinking can boost your success and happiness ten times. All I ask is that when I share this with you, you make no judgement for now. You just read this book and follow the steps I give you, and once you have finished, you can make your judgement then. Is that a deal?

OK. Here it is. Enter the *Universe*.

I've made it clear that I'm not religious. But I do believe in a Universal Intelligence and what in some hoods is referred to as G-DOG or God. OK, nobody calls it G-DOG but hey, sue me, sometimes a girl likes to channel her inner gangster. In fact, I love to see myself as a bit of a spiritual badass breaking all the rules of what I once thought a spiritual person had to be. I'm like 50 per cent Deepak and 50 per cent Tupac.

When I was little, I distinctly remember feeling confused and asking my mother a perplexing question. What was inside me that could see out of my eyes? I knew there was something inside my body that was looking outward but as a child I could not comprehend it. I knew that if I closed my eyes I could still hear a voice inside my head.

As humans we exist in multiple dimensions at the same time. There is a physical part of us: the part you see in the mirror and that interacts with other physical forms such as humans, objects and so on. This part is of us is tangible and takes physical action in the physical world. There is also another part to us. Our non-physical, inner essence that fuels and gives life to our physical being, which is made up of our thoughts, feelings and beliefs. Both the physical and non-physical realms of our existence are inseparable, like the top and the bottom of our foot.

Spirituality is the practice of connection with that non-physical part of you. As humans, we have been accustomed to an 'outside-in' approach to judging how happy we are, which then sets the tone for the journey of our life towards a destination that will never really fulfil us. For me, spirituality is remembering what you are: a motherfucking superstar. It's the sacred practice of going inward to realize your own potential. It's also the unwavering faith that there is something out there that truly does have your back on this journey of life and will be there to hold your hand every step of the way, if you let it.

Let me clear up some myths about what it means to be a spiritual person. I don't wear bamboo trousers; I don't own a lotus leaf; I'm most likely to be found chanting 'fuck' instead of 'Om', and yes, I shave my armpits. I used to believe that being spiritual was for people who weren't normal. After years of being bullied and ever so desperately trying to fit in (so much so that I begged my mum to change my name by deed poll), I felt like anything 'out there' was not even something I would contemplate and would hugely interfere with my perpetual quest to be totally average. And while I'm being entirely candid here, even the word 'spiritual' made me cringe … a lot! But my life needed to change, and quite frankly I was willing to be open to anything because what I had been doing wasn't working.

If you can understand and harness the power of the Universe in your quest for transformation, you will find the journey ten times easier and bucket-loads more joyful. You can read all the success books on mindset in the world, but the secret is to utilize the incredible energy source right at your fingertips to make those dreams a reality.

I am going to talk in a lot more depth in the following chapter about how and why the Universe can amplify your success, but I need you to just trust me here. When we bring psychology and spirituality together, it creates a marriage like no other and opens the floodgates for *magic* in your life. My life radically upgraded when I started on my journey of personal development but even more so when I began my spiritual journey and became obsessed with creating the life of my dreams by understanding and implementing the fundamentals I teach in this book. The reason why I believe this is not only because I have experienced it myself but also because I have seen it in hundreds of clients and colleagues. If you can tap into this invisible, sweet, loving Universal Intelligence that makes shit happen in the world, you will make your success stratospheric. This is what spirituality is all about. Scout's honour. Guide's honour. Cross my heart and hope to die.

I want this book to be your spiritual and psychological washing machine. I want it to cleanse you of all the bullshit that you have had emblazoned on to your brain. I want it to help you pull out the paint palette, refill it with every freaking colour and guide you to paint the most fantastical picture that would make even Picasso look like an amateur. Look, it's no easy feat to battle against decades of conditioning and I need you to promise me something.

You must make an absolute and utter commitment to do a few things:

- Make a daily commitment to your personal development.
- Read every last bit of this book and everything I teach.
- Implement the tasks in each chapter. They will create change beyond your beliefs.
- Send me a bottle of Prosecco.

OK, I'm kidding about the last one but just checking you are still with me. Above all, I categorically need you to be open to a new perspective.

Changing lives

Books have radically changed my life, and I want this book to change yours. I remember sitting in a coffee shop back in 2012 in the middle of winter, freezing cold and heavily pregnant. I had just thrown up again after another bout of morning sickness, and after deciding to skip work, I found solace in the warmth of a hot chocolate. I opened up a book that I had found on my mother's bookshelf. The book was called *Think and Grow Rich* by Napoleon Hill, and never in a million years (until that moment) did I think that a book could change the trajectory of my life.

This book taught me something that I'd never been shown before. I was trying not to splutter my hot chocolate everywhere in shock as I frantically turned the pages, devouring every word with an utter passion as it taught me about the power of my mind. Could this be real? They had clearly forgotten to teach this stuff to me in the private school that my mum had been duped into paying thousands for so that I could learn about Henry VIII's wives and how rain was made in clouds.

I mean those things are good to know, but they were never going to change my life. The words inside this book would.

I felt a mixture of anger and excitement. Anger that in 15 years of education no one had felt the need to mention an approach that *could change my whole life*. I started googling away and became a fully-fledged Universe Junkie. I remember that day in the coffee shop like it was yesterday. I remember the sense of possibility that I had never felt before in my life and I can honestly say, when I cast my mind back in time, I barely recognize myself as I was then – hopeless, lost and desperate for a way out of her sucky life.

Perhaps you are that person in the coffee shop. Or perhaps you're not her at all, and you have got your shit together, but you know there's more shit to get done. Or maybe you're the person who doesn't have a clue what they want to do with their life. Or perhaps you have success outwardly but feel bank-rupt internally and don't understand why, because you've real-ized that Jimmy Choo and Range Rover haven't brought you the joy you thought they would. Whatever your story, this book will show you where things have been going wrong and how you can systematically change them.

When I look back on the past few years of my life and then cast my mind back to the decade before, it is pretty incred-ible. I think back to the girl who suffered anxiety, yoyoed with depression, spent most of her days judging herself and others, and felt lost. The scary thing was that on the outside my life looked good and I was having fun, but inside, I was a chronic giver-upper and well-trained life escape artist. I was just good at putting on a show.

So ...

- It's time to move past the fear of failure and the fear of the unknown.
- It's time to stop living life with a comparison hangover.
- It's time to step into your power as the incredible and amazing person that you were born to be.
- It's time to start loving yourself and believing in yourself in a way you never thought possible.
- It's time to say goodbye to the excuses about not having enough time and/or energy.

If it was possible for me, I believe it's possible for you, too! I'm just a regular girl who learned how to turn the impossible into the possible, and I did this all with the help of the principles in this book and my BFF, the Universe. Sometimes it takes a decade to get to the one year that really changes your life. Are you ready to make this your year?

So, let's start this journey.

TOP TAKEAWAYS
. . . .

- Where you are now is not where you can be in a week, month or year.
- Psychology is incredibly vital in changing your life, and it all starts with your mind.
- When you bring the Universe into the equation, you can skyrocket your success. Making the Universe your BFF is your secret weapon.
- Don't judge until you have got through the whole book and implemented all the tasks and actions.
- You need to commit to your transformation for this all to work.

JFDI!

Trust the Universe

Let's get to your first task, which I did after reading Pam Grout's book *E-Squared* (2013). In order for you to trust me, you need to see proof. After all, the proof of the pudding is in the eating. So, let's test the Universe. The rules are simple, but you absolutely *must* abide by them. You promised me earlier, remember, that you would come with an open mind and leave judgement at the door until the end of the book.

The rules:

1 For the next 24 hours, I need you to put aside any doubt, any second-guessing and to FULLY BELIEVE that the Universe is your BFF and will help you to co-create. I am only asking you to commit to 24 hours (for now).

2 I want you to find a quiet spot and repeat this after me OUT LOUD. You can adapt, but you get the idea.
   'Hi Universe, I need to believe that you have my back, like really believe in you, so I need you to do me a favour. I need you to show me that you are listening. I need you to give me a gift within the next 24 hours. You choose, but let it be a surprise. And also tell me that it's you with a nudge of knowing, so I really know it is from YOU.'

3 OK, now your job is to LOOK for the gift. Yep, don't forget you asked the Universe, and you need to EXPECT it is coming. You need to KNOW – 100 per cent with all your belief – that it is happening. When you go to a restaurant and order your meal, you have confidence and expectation that your food will arrive. You are ordering a gift from the Universe, and you must exercise this exact expectation.

4 Sit back and wait for the gift.

Follow these rules explicitly and watch how the Universe delivers. The gift may only be small, but remember something that comes as a surprise within 24 hours is the gift you have been waiting for. I even got my husband to do this task once. He reluctantly participated in asking for a gift. The next day he was tidying up and he was excited to find a remote that had been missing for weeks. He was so happy and said that he just couldn't believe it – he thought it was gone for good. I looked at him and reminded him of the task we had done the day before. I smiled, and he became a total believer.

Now it's your turn. Follow the rules and watch the magic unfold.

2

It's All About the Vibes

Vibrational mastery will be your new hobby – after all, knitting is so 2011.

I remember the first time I fell in love. Like madly and completely in love. I was nine. I was at summer camp for two weeks, and this is where I learned my first lessons about love and me.

His name was Vinnie. He was eight and kind of round with dark hair, but something about him just lit me up. I remember the excitement of seeing him and the sadness I felt at parting.

More than all of that, I remember being ballsy. I had no fear when it came to expressing my feelings, and I was apparently a born romantic brainwashed by Disney from an incredibly young age.

I picked the perfect moment to deliver my Oscar-winning declaration, which took place towards the end of the two weeks, under water at the local leisure centre. I mean you can't get much more romantic than that.

As I signalled for Vinnie to go under water next to the supersize multi-coloured inflatable, I held my breath and was poised as I lowered myself under the water. I began frantically pointing to my eyes, then led his gaze to where I was tapping my heart, which I followed with the finishing touch of pointing at him.

'I LOVE YOU!' I mouthed, and, boy, I did.

I honestly cannot remember what happened at that point. I want to say he did something similar back, but I have probably repressed the rejection with the pile of others I received in the years after. It didn't last longer than the summer camp and I was only nine, but I never forgot about my first summer love affair.

He lived in a different town and there was no chance of us meeting again but I spent days and nights daydreaming about my first love. Three years later, I moved to a new house and it turned out to be in the same road as Vinnie's.

A decade later, I met him again in a pub where, in a drunken stupor, he proudly related the story to all his friends about how I declared my undying love under water. The cringe factor was so unbearable, it almost took my breath away.

Maybe you will think this was one hell of a coincidence. However, there is also a strong possibility that, given what I will share in this chapter, you may begin to see the power of energy in action and how our thoughts give the Universe a heads-up in creating our physical reality. I am pretty sure that I 'manifested' my whole family moving to a new house so that I could be reunited with Vinnie. Oops. Sorry, Mum.

What the fuck is 'manifesting'?

So, let me break this down for you, because understanding the principles behind manifesting is essential. When you manifest, you have brought into reality something that you once thought of.

This is called the Law of Attraction, and this, simply put, means that you can attract what you want into your life – because your thoughts can absolutely become your physical reality. It is a *universal* law, which means it works for *everyone, all of the time*, whether we are aware of it or not and we can't be messing with laws! I remember how, when I was growing up, my mother would always tell me that I could do anything that I put my mind to. She was right, but there's a whole dimension to it that I never really understood.

The Law of Attraction states that we can attract anything we want if we truly desire it. Everything in our physical world – our bodies, relationships, finances – is a direct reflection of our internal state and thoughts. Simply put, how you feel on the inside will mirror what you see on the outside. Your perception of the outer world is directly correlated to your internal world. What this means is that, whether we are conscious of it or not, we are responsible for bringing both positive and negative influences into our lives.

This isn't some woo-woo nonsense. As humans, we rely so much on the notion that what we see with our eyes is reality that we can all be excused for not really appreciating what exists beyond that. There are many forms of energy waves within the electromagnetic spectrum – radio, light, sound, infrared, ultra-violet, gamma to name but a few. They exist all around us and can be measured with scientific instruments yet are invisible to the human eye. This means that we must open our minds to what we cannot see. Gravity is not visible, yet we can feel it holding us down to the ground. We can't see electricity, but we know not to stick our fingers into a plug socket. Having faith in the Law of Attraction means having confidence in the invisible forces that are working tirelessly around us.

Take a moment to think about your physical world and everything tangible in it – cars, houses, people, a freezer full of Ben and Jerry's – OK, maybe that's just me. Before the car came the idea of the car. Before the house was built came the *desire* to build the house. Before Ben and Jerry made tubs of delicious, ridiculously high-calorie ice cream came the *thought* of building an ice cream empire. Everything that is now in the *physical* world started off as a thought, a daydream or a desire.

Of course, I'm not negating the fact that you need to take action. A car didn't magically appear in a puff of smoke straight after the idea was conceived like some Harry Potter piece of wizardry. A business doesn't automatically make a million dollars just because someone desired it and thought about it. Our physical bodies must take action alongside the non-physical Universal Intelligence. It's this Universal Intelligence that is helping us along the way by providing us with the right opportunities and insights to bring our ideas to physical fruition with ease.

Once you have thought of something in your mind, the Universal Intelligence will use its energy to make it happen for you. If you have been fantasizing about a new partner in life, once that vision has been secured in your mind, the Universe will help create the circumstances in which you meet that person. If you can think about it, then it can always be manifested into physical reality. The idea has been given to you because it

JUST F*CKING DO IT

is *meant* for you. The desire has been given to you because it is meant for you. If you can see it in your mind, then you have the power to make it a reality. Isn't that cool? But it's crucial that you understand that, although thoughts are creative, not all thoughts are equally creative. Do you get everything you think about? No you don't, and thank goodness. I mean, imagine if every thought of a teenage boy became reality – the world would be totally messed up!

Many of the thoughts people think never materialize, because they lack many of the ingredients necessary for turning them into physical reality. Most thoughts don't possess enough strength to cause things to happen. There is not enough ambition, desire and belief behind them, and the thoughts are not repeated often enough to gain the power to cause movement in the energy. Whatever you put your attention to will grow as long as you are feeding lots of positive energy in its direction. Desire and attention give energy to the Law of Attraction, which then literally turns you into a magnet for your desires and transports all you want from the non-physical world of thought into the physical world.

Some things take longer for the Universe to orchestrate while some thoughts manifest quickly and easily even without much energy or focus. Have you ever thought about someone and then suddenly they telephoned out of the blue? Some may call this coincidence, chance or luck. But I believe it's the Universe showing you that what you think can come to fruition.

So, what is the Universal Intelligence?

Physics shows us that the entire universe is the movement of energy and information, and at some level everything is made up of the same raw materials – carbon, oxygen and nitrogen.

Imagine a tomato. A beautiful, juicy red tomato. Where did it come from? Can I hear you saying, 'a seed'? Well, if you went and got some of those seeds and rubbed them between your fingers for long enough, what would happen to them? They would disintegrate into dust. If you put that dust under a microscope, you wouldn't see any magical tomato-growing molecules; you would just see the same atoms that we and every thing else are made of.

We are made of the same stuff as tomato seed dust, but something causes that dust to turn into beautiful yummy red tomatoes, a stupendous energy force. It's the same energy force that takes our thoughts and turns them into physical reality. The same energy that makes our hair and nails grow and helps us to breathe every day. We take all this stuff so much for granted that we don't stop to question *how* it actually happens.

Ultimately, we are made of the same stuff as a chair, a tree, the tomato and even that smelly stray sock you regularly find under your bed. Just lots of energy particles vibrating. It's a revelation that blew my mind. So, in essence, we are all just walking, talking, thinking – and hopefully not stinking – socks. OK, I may have gone too far with that, but it made me chuckle.

The seed is the potential of a big tomato – it is the 'idea' behind the tomato. With good faith, we know that, if we plant that seed, water it and give it sun … boom, a tomato will appear! We don't doubt that the seed will turn into a tomato. We have a belief that it will grow, even if we have never asked ourselves what actually causes it to grow. Well, that incredible force of power is the formless energy and the intelligence behind life, referred to as many different things in different hoods – the Source, God, Mother Nature, the Motherload, Allah, the Goddess or the Life Force.

They all refer to the same thing, a powerful-as-fuck energy that turns ideas into reality. I refer to this invisible force as the Universe throughout this book. The Universe is taking our mental pictures and helping us turn them into our perfect jobs, dream cars, Mulberry handbags and ideal partners. Having faith in this invisible force of nature will help you transform your life more quickly then you ever would have otherwise because it gives you the comfort of knowing that you don't have to go on the journey alone and that you can deliberately co-create your life. So, as you can see, the long and short of manifestation is *energy*.

Whether you like it or not, believe it or not, this energy is always working in the background. Whether you are trying to lose weight, find the love of your life or make more money, there are tangible, practical ways you can change your mindset from a psychological perspective to make this happen, and I will be sharing these all with you throughout this book. However, having the knowledge that you can create what you want, if you truly want it, and design a life of your dreams is pretty amazing.

So, how the heck do you manifest what you want?

Let me start by saying that, although there are some clear steps to deliberately creating your life (aka manifesting), it's also a process that is natural for us – once you have been through this whole book and have begun to unleash your potential, you will find that manifesting becomes more natural and less a step-by-step procedure.

I once heard an explanation that really illustrated this well. Let's say that you went to a school as a child where you learned about manifesting and the notion of manifesting became so normal that you didn't even question it. The belief was supported by your parents, your teachers and your peers, and therefore you knew that, if you desired something and took action, it would be yours. Your beliefs would be different and your outlook on life would be dramatically different.

The first step to manifesting is to *decide what you really want.* Chapter 3 will be all about goal setting and will help you craft your ideal life. The second step is to *decide that it's done*, which means having complete faith in the Law of Attraction. This is the hard part, as your brain will fight you on this, because you didn't in fact go to the school of manifesting, so you need to train your mind and reprogram it to believe it. Expectation is a powerful force because it gives you the confidence that you can create the life you desire. The more you see things happening in your life and the more you witness your thoughts manifesting, this will start giving you the confidence and helping you believe that this shizzle is, in fact, very real.

In the JFDI! task at the end of Chapter 1, I told you for 24 hours to expect the Universe to give you a gift, with the same level of expectation that your food would arrive at a restaurant. Imagine you did go to that school where manifesting was drummed into you. As you make your way through this book and start seeing things change, your faith in the power of manifesting will increase and your 'faith muscle' will get stronger. Instead of questioning whether the outcome will come to fruition, you will take inspired action in the *full knowledge* and *expectation* that the outcome will be yours.

We will cover what 'inspired action' means later on, too. In order for you to take inspired action, you need to understand what deep-rooted beliefs you have that are in conflict with what you desire, and how to reprogram them. (We will tackle this very soon.)

Being a vibrational master – how to stay tuned to UniverseFM

One of the most important pieces of the puzzle, so that we can manifest like a mofo, is taking control of how we feel. The way you feel gives off a vibration. Have you ever referred to someone as 'high vibe' or 'low vibe'? Well, as humans we can literally feel the vibrations of those around us. When we feel joy, love, freedom, gratitude and passion we literally vibrate at a higher frequency, and when we feel fear, depression, grief, insecurity and guilt we vibrate at a much lower frequency.

In order to manifest, we need to be in vibrational alignment with the Universe. To know for sure whether we are in alignment and whether the vibration we are putting out is attracting what we want, not pushing it away, we need to pay close attention to how we feel.

Imagine owning a radio and UniverseFM being the channel you need to be tuned in to in order to manifest. UniverseFM has a high vibrational frequency. In general, when we feel good, we are in 'attraction' mode and tuned in to UniverseFM, and when we feel bad, we are tuned in to a frequency of lack – let's call this ShitFM. The better we feel, the more open we are for our desires to come to us easily. Simply stated, our emotions are the biggest indicator of whether we are in alignment.

Have you ever noticed that some people seem to have it all and are so 'lucky' because they keep just getting more and more amazing stuff? Conversely, cast your mind back to one of those days where one thing after another kept going wrong. There is no such thing as coincidence. It is all down to your energy creating everything that your mind is vibrationally putting out there, and that is exactly how the Law of Attraction works.

Let's step away from energy and look at this from a psychological perspective. If you desire something, feeling happy and energized and in the 'right frame of mind' is going to help you take action towards getting it. Numerous academic studies show that happy individuals are successful across multiple areas of their life including marriage, friendship, income, work performance and health. Psychologists also argue that the happiness–success link exists not only because success makes people happy, but also because a positive disposition fuels success.

Once upon a time, when I first stumbled across the Law of Attraction, I was willing to believe anything despite my cynical mindset at that time. I tried to manifest £100k but didn't realize that there is a process to activating the Law of Attraction that one must follow. I just sat on my arse eating tortilla chips wondering why, as soon as it became apparent that the £100k wasn't coming my way, the Universe hated me. The reality is, I wasn't in the right of frame of mind; I was firmly tuned in to ShitFM. I was never going to attract anything (or do anything to make that £100k) when my energy was so low vibe and so I quickly pooh-poohed the whole concept.

Managing your energy is the number-one rule of manifesting our desires, and this is one of the hardest things for us as humans to do. Why? Because for so long we have been letting our overly conditioned subconscious run the show and are too easily influenced by what is going on around us in the physical world rather than tapping into our highest potential. Our emotions are often a by-product of the situations happening around us, the impact of other humans on us and our subconscious limiting our thought patterns.

So how do we start changing our energy so that we are constantly tuned in to UniverseFM? How do we stay happy and joyful and high energy all the time? Well, look, we are humans and I am realistic; sometimes things happen that just piss us off, like getting a parking ticket, or disagreeing with the mother-in-law (again). But, seriously, there are ways to manage our energy so that we can bounce back quickly if we do accidentally find ourselves tuned in to ShitFM and belting out a tune to 'crap, crap, crap'. And sometimes, really bad things do happen in our lives that knock us for six and then we spiral into a low-vibe state.

It's your job, however, to become super-conscious of yourself (this book will help you do that) so that even in those moments when you feel anger, rage, jealousy, envy or any other negative emotion creep up, you know how to quickly shift your energy back to a positive state. This doesn't mean repressing or ignoring negative emotions. They are just as important in our lives as positive ones as they provide us with valuable data. We need to feel the full range of what is going on internally for two reasons:

1 When we feel down or frustrated or going through something challenging, we can use that as a marker for what we don't want. How many success stories have you heard where there's a rags-to-riches theme? It often takes someone to hit rock bottom before they can feel a whole-hearted desire to make a huge change.

2 When we go through difficult times in our lives, it shows us where we need to grow more resilience, confidence and gusto. It gives us the opportunity to see if we are playing the victim.

Understand this: pain is physical, but suffering is mental, and that even in the worst times of our lives, we always have a choice to think differently. Being positive isn't mumbo-jumbo – we really can choose to see every situation through a different lens, one with a solution.

I know that my dreams and desires rely on me staying high-vibe and I have turned achieving this into an art form. And I want you to make this an art, too. Vibrational mastery will be your new hobby – after all, knitting is so 2011. By the time you have finished this book, you will have all the tools of the perfect vibrational master, and you will be something akin to a superhero. And although I know that, however much I dream of it, I won't ever be able to fly without the aid of some as yet un-invented jetpack, I do believe that we humans can achieve a level of vibrational mastery that allows us to manifest some crazy stuff.

So how do we become masters of vibration and tap into attracting what we want like a magician? (And just for the record, I finally did manifest that £100k in one month – this stuff really does work.)

Clear your connection

The first step is that I want you to imagine a tunnel of light that goes straight up from the top of your head towards a big ball of yellow energy. (Have you ever done that in a yoga class?) That big ball of yellow energy is the centre of the Universe. Well, that tunnel of light needs to be a bright white for us to be able to manifest what we want. And I hate to break this to you, for so many people it is black – yes, *black*! However, in most cases, while black is my colour of choice for outerwear, when it comes to my connection to the Universe, it needs to be bright, bright white.

That blackness arises out of years of conditioning, comparing, judging, criticizing and complaining. Hands up if you're guilty! Heck, we *all* are, and if you are there shaking your head, then you may as well give up right now on this transforming-your-life malarkey because being honest with yourself is step numero uno. Your job is to clear out that tunnel so you can have a direct, clear, efficient access to the Universe that allows you to manifest your deepest desires.

So how do we clear up our connection to the Universe? Well, we need to understand a few things going on inside us that have corroded the tunnel and turned it black. Let's start with the fact that, even though we are one person, we have different levels of operating.

Firstly, as I have explained earlier in the book, we can operate from a conscious level and from a subconscious level. And scarily, over 80 per cent of what we do comes from the subconscious. The brain conserves energy by 'automating' our day-to-day processes and thinking. Remember, our brain is simply an organ that acts like a computer, storing and processing data.

Secondly we can operate from a place of Ego or from a place of Higher Wisdom, or what I will refer to as Soul. I am going to keep this explanation of Ego in its most simplistic form and purely from a spiritual rather than psychological perspective. The Ego is the 'thought' part of you, and its voice is made up of society's conditioning and past experiences. Its default state has evolved to being fear, and more often than not our Ego voice becomes rooted in irrationality. The Ego creates an illusion based on your human experiences and negates the fact that there is a part of you that isn't rooted in the physical world. As we go through life, we believe its voice to be the truth because it is the loudest in our mind. The description given by Sogyal Rinpoche in *The Tibetan Book of Living and Dying* is a brilliant explanation: 'Two people have been living in you all of your life. One is the ego, garrulous, demanding, hysterical, calculating; the other is the hidden spiritual being, whose still voice of wisdom you have only rarely heard or attended to.'

Back when I was at university I lived in a student house with my best friend. She made me laugh, always made me feel good about myself and loved me just for who I was. We decided to get a new housemate, and someone we knew jumped at the chance to live with us. But things took a turn for the worse pretty quickly. The new housemate was negative and always seemed to focus on the worst aspect of things. She lowered the vibe and we always felt on edge around her.

We used to chip in for obligatory household things like toilet paper. On one particular occasion, this obnoxious housemate made some pretty serious allegations about my best friend's excessive use of toilet paper. She accused her of using too much and insisted that she cut down to just one or two sheets per session! Of course, we found this hilarious that our housemate had such a scarcity mindset that loo roll rationing became a thing in our house. However, her constant irrational demands made us feel like we had to go around treading on eggshells.

Ego is the loo-paper police in full action! The Ego has you running from pillar to post convincing you that happiness is to be found elsewhere *outside* of you. It likes to talk about wanting material things and will convince you that going out and acquiring material objects will bring you happiness. Ironically, once you have acquired the 'stuff' it will then then tell you it isn't enough. It will often also consider the worst-case scenario, look to blame others for personal unhappiness, and judge all those around. The Ego voice always likes to be right, hates being questioned and loves to feel victimized. The Ego convinces you to be selfish and only look out for yourself because life – according to the Ego – is for working, suffering and then dying. It has you running around life like a headless chicken on a mission for success that it has no intention of letting you complete. The Ego will tell you that nobody likes you, that you aren't good-looking enough and that your bottom is too big. In short, it's a bit of an asshole.

At this level of being, we simply go through life with our thoughts guiding us on autopilot without ever questioning what our real purpose is or truly tapping into our true potential.

We must transcend this rudimentary level of living if we are to feel true happiness and manifest our dream life. At the next level, we become conscious and we start to realize that thoughts are just thoughts, just data being pushed out of our brain (which is an operating system), and that we can change our thoughts at any given second, if we start to become aware of them. This then allows us to start running from a very different level, the level of *Soul*.

The majority of people are on the Ego setting and my job is to help you flip the switch to the Soul setting. At this level, you begin to realize that you are connected to the Universal Intelligence and you have the power to manifest. When your Soul switch is flicked on, instead of going through life with fear, you begin to recognize that you have unbounded potential and life is full of limitless possibilities. Your Soul, if you like, is the divine part of you that is connected with the Universe. It's there to look after you spiritually and emotionally, and often communicates without words. While the Ego voice is strong and authoritative in your mind, the voice of your Soul 'speaks' more softly and quietly. It may often communicate in subtle ways at first but can also become persistent or nagging. When you are connected to this divine part of you, everything seems to make sense and there is a feeling of inner knowledge. Soul sees life only through the lens of love and is proudly opting to go through life with a spangly pair of rose-tinted glasses.

Your Soul knows that you are amazing even without any of the material things that the Ego wants you to work your butt off for. It gently hugs you and nudges you with intuition and inspiration to let you know that your ideas matter and that you have big things to do on this planet and it will guide you with your best interests at heart.

For much of your life, the Ego, like that obnoxious housemate, has made all the noise and has had you going through life on eggshells. As you grow older, your Ego becomes stronger and an even bigger loudmouth. It dampens out the voice of your Soul.

In order to clear that blackened tunnel and reignite your connection to the Universe, you need to become totally aware and determine who is running the show at any given moment in your life. There is a constant battle between Ego and Soul, but once you move on to a level of conscious awareness (something most humans never ever do), your life will regain an incredible sense of power.

When our lives are led under the leadership and guidance of our Soul, our energy will automatically skyrocket. We learn to stop judging, comparing, criticizing and start loving, forgiving, being grateful and living with joy. When ruled by the Ego you will swear at the dude who cuts you up on the road instead of letting him pass with a smile, knowing that a moment longer waiting doesn't matter. The Ego will be forever telling you stories of how you aren't ever going to be a success (so don't bother with that new venture!), yet your Soul, just like your best friend, will keep nudging you with inspiration the whole way and cheer you along the journey. When you lead your life with love, you are leading from your Soul. When you lead it through fear, that's Ego's bullshit.

People often ask me how I have manifested such amazing things, and I will be sharing the exact process of how I myself changed throughout the book, but it all started with my becoming aware of my thoughts and choosing to lead with love and to ignore that pesky, menacing Ego. Once you start recognizing who is running the show, you can begin adjusting your energy to ensure that you are running on the high-vibe energy of love. I began to observe my thoughts and realized that I could choose to change them at any given moment. Humans are lucky because we are capable of training our minds so that we become consciously aware of the energy and information that we want to create or un-create in our lives. We are energy: everything we manifest is just energy.

But let me tell you, changing things can feel really hard. Changing our mindset, becoming acutely aware of our thoughts and actions, is probably one of the most difficult things we can do, but it is the secret to unlocking the power of long-lasting transformation and allowing happiness to infiltrate our lives. I know now that by eliminating hatred, envy, jealousy, selfishness and cynicism, and by developing a love for even the most annoying person, and most importantly, for myself, I can achieve what I want because this is me tuning in to UniverseFM.

I know that a negative attitude towards others can never bring me the success I desire, and I want that success. The question is: how much do you want it?

Let's say you wake up on the wrong side of the bed, moaning that it's Monday morning and that you have to take your booty back to the job you hate. This immediately puts you in a bad mood. This energy is not conducive to attaining anything you want in life as it is low frequency – you've tuned in to

ShitFM, but at that moment you have the choice to change it. You can put some Beyoncé on, dance around the room like a looney, and remind yourself that you are amazing and have the power to change your life. By changing your thoughts, you change your emotions, which in turn shifts your energy and guides your actions. Now you can focus on your 9–5 escape plan instead of dwelling on the situation you are in right now.

As you can see, changing your mindset is crucial if you are to activate the Law of Attraction. The Law of Attraction encourages you to see that you have the freedom to take control of how your future develops, shaping it in the ways you choose. That is pretty exciting stuff.

But whether you totally buy into it or not, in essence, the big message here is that, when we feel good, we can make so much more happen in our lives. When we choose to stop seeing life through a negative lens, we open up a world of possibility. And the crux of this is, you can *choose*. You can choose to think differently and feel differently. What this means for you is that you can have total control of your life, if you want it. That you no longer need to have any sort of belief that you are stuck where you are or destined for a life that is run by your childhood conditioning.

TOP TAKEAWAYS

- When you manifest, you have brought into reality something that you once thought of.
- In order to manifest you must be tuned in to UniverseFm and vibrating at a high frequency.
- In order to be 'high vibe' you must be aware of how you feel and learn to control it.
- Ego is the fear-based part of you that has been created from childhood conditioning.
- Your Soul is the loving and powerful part of you that is directly connected to the Universal Intelligence.

JFDI!

Role-playing with the Universe

This is a hack to changing your energy. When you can tune in to the energy of the biggest bad-assed version of yourself, you can shift your vibration. The quickest way to manifest is to make sure that your energy is *now* in alignment with that of UniverseFM even if your situation doesn't quite match your desired reality. Thinking and acting in accordance with your future instead of your current reality may seem mind-boggling but will immediately teach you how to think about things differently.

Take a moment to imagine yourself ten years down the line with *everything* you desire: the money, the partner of your dreams (or living the singleton life), a fit and toned healthy body with no illness, a family that loves you, friendships that fulfil you, and let's throw in a private jet for good measure.

I want you to imagine yourself as really, really happy, feeling emotionally, mentally and physically fulfilled. That 'future self' you can see in your mind will be vibrating at a really high frequency because it is the best, happiest, most fulfilled version of yourself. Feel the energy inside you shift as you see yourself in your mind's eye stepping into your biggest life.

Now write down five things you would *feel*, five things you would *believe* and five things you would *think* if it was done, if you were the person you dream of becoming. You can use the note section at the end of this book to write this down.

That is the vibration you need to bring into everyday life.

You can hack your manifesting by summoning those five feelings, five beliefs and five thoughts into the present moment. When you do, you will become a magnet for the positive energies of the Universe, helping you to realize your ideal future self.

3

Think It, Get It #Goaldigger

Don't downgrade your dreams, upgrade your belief baby.

I remember sheepishly telling my career advisor at school that I wanted to be an actress – or, to be honest, anything that could involve me being on stage performing. I was sheepish because of the countless times people had told me it wasn't realistic and offered no stability. I had been convinced within an inch of my soul that what I wanted wasn't achievable. It was all so blah, blah, blah. Every time anybody talked about my future, it felt as if my dreams were being pushed further and further away. Maybe you can relate to this?

So, guess what this taught me as a child? Don't have goals. Don't dream big. Stop sharing any goals that people are likely to say are not achievable. Stay realistic, stay comfortable, stay ordinary.

That was the message that was drummed into me and no doubt you know exactly what I am talking about. My goals in life became very focused on what everyone else was doing, what everyone wanted for me and what I thought was acceptable in society. I had stopped listening to my intuition, stopped fighting for my dreams, and I felt like Nemo desperately trying to find his way home.

A significant part of the Law of Attraction is understanding that where you place your focus and energy has a massive impact on what happens to you. In this chapter, I'll share with you how to make goals that turn you on and how to go about getting them even if they feel far out of reach. I want you to feel comfortable with setting goals that make you feel hot under the collar and may even make you slightly cringe, because then you know you are being true to yourself and letting yourself dream *really* big.

Your goals need to mean something to you

Goals give you a sense of direction that removes that feeling of overwhelm, and when you have a plan of action in place to make those goals happen, well … the world is your mother-fucking oyster. So many people I meet ask me the same question, and it's a question I have also asked myself a dozen times: 'What am I supposed to do with my life?' As humans we have needs, and besides our basic needs for food, shelter and love, we all have a desire to grow. As outlined in Maslow's hierarchy of needs, we have a desire 'to become everything one is capable of becoming'.

Humans need to feel as if they have a purpose. We want success. Success comes in various shapes and forms and is by no means merely monetary – at the beginning of this book I wrote that, for me, success is feeling happy and free. All the things I do in my life allow me the choice to do what I want and give my life meaning, and that is *my* way of being successful.

But what does success mean to you? It is mind-blowing how small a number of people actually sit down to think about what they want. This is the first piece of the puzzle in changing your life, and I want you to take a moment now to sit in silence and to think about what your dream life looks like. Where do you live? What do you do? How much money do you earn? Are you married? Do you have kids? Perhaps you live alone in a beach-front hut in Thailand or have married a flamenco dancer in Ecuador. But whatever your dream life is, I want you to take a few moments to ask yourself: what does being successful mean to you? How does it *feel*?

If you got in a car and started driving aimlessly around with no destination in mind, you would waste fuel and get frustrated. One of our primary human needs for survival is growth, and, if we aren't progressing, we are left with internal friction. When we lack purpose and direction, we plod through life, and this lack of fulfilment can manifest itself in anxiety, depression, anger, physical illness and a love of class A drugs (been there, done that, and got the comedown scars to prove it).

And even 'successful' people can go through these emotions and experiences if their goals are mostly driven by material gain. There are many celebrities out there who outwardly have the trappings of success – the money, the cars, the houses, the fame – yet the media is filled with stories of addiction and breakdown. Why? Because these people have focused on a kind of success that is fixated on material gain, following the lead of Ego and sacrificing other parts of their life. And, ultimately, this leads to the same ending for so many – crash and burn and then rehab. I don't want that for you. I want you to have desires that will fill up your Soul and make you happy. I want you to become the best version of yourself, not just strive to make one part of your life better.

What is also important is that your goals are yours. Trust me, lots of people have goals that aren't theirs. There are plenty of people who have goals based on what will make their parents proud, make society look up to them or what they perceive to be the right thing to do, despite the fact that these goals make them miserable. These are precisely the types of goals that I don't want you to have.

Goal setting like a boss

I am going to show you not only how to set goals that you are obsessed with so that you achieve them, but I also want you to use your secret weapon – the Universe!

So where do you start with setting goals?

Firstly, you do need to know where you are going. Your internal GPS requires a destination to be inputted. You need total clarity on what success means for you and an understanding of what it will feel and look like once you have got there.

Don't forget: vibrational mastery is what we want. So, the reason so many people stay stuck in a rut of perpetual 'not knowing what to do-ness' is because they are scared of letting their imaginations run wild and dreaming of all the possibilities. They are burdened with the questions of 'How will it ever happen?' instead of basking in the magic and excitement of what could be possible for them.

With that in mind, begin by grabbing a piece of paper, or using the notes section at the end of this book, and being really honest about what you want. Answer this: what would your deepest desire be for your life, even if you had no idea how to make it happen? I really need to you to take any thoughts of being realistic out of this. Take the 'how?' out of it. Just write. I just want you to *revel* in your desire.

Even if you don't know the exact details, you just need an idea of what you want your life to look like and, most importantly, how you want to feel. Remember that this isn't rigid and can change. The JFDI! exercise at the end of this chapter will help you get clarity on this, but just know that, once you are clear about your goals, events will start happening to make that a reality – that is, if you follow all the steps I'll be showing you!

If you are grappling with the above question, think about the things you aren't happy or satisfied with currently. This will be a great start. Perhaps you don't like your job, or you are done with being single at Christmas or dislike the fact that you have to rummage through clearance sections at the supermarket. Sometimes it is easier to start with what we don't like and then use that as a measure of what you want to change.

Not everyone has massive goals to change the world, and that is totally OK. Remember, success is whatever you define it to be and that changes from person to person. However, it is important to decide on what you want and then give it the attention and love it deserves to make it a reality. For the Law of Attraction to work, attention is critical, so setting really excellent goals gives your mind somewhere to focus. Whatever you focus on, things will start to happen.

Let me share how my life unfolded and what chang.. for me. In the winter of 2013, I was sitting in my car crying like a baby outside my daughter's nursery. I had left my 14-month-old for the first time with a bunch of strangers. I distinctly remember having such a strong desire in my heart that my life needed to change so that I could leave my job and be with my little girl.

The thing is, I still had no clue what was going to happen. My goal at the time was merely that something had to change and that I wanted help to find out how to change it. I wanted to feel freedom.

I want you to absorb this sentence. Sometimes you don't need to know the finer details; you just need to know how you want to feel as a result and let the Universe point you in the right direction. That is precisely what happened to me, and the following few years transpired to be my most spectacular. The low moment for me provided me with a benchmark of what I wanted to change.

You see, when we feel lost and confused, if we try to figure things out logically, we can hit resistance when we are not quite sure about the exact details. Resistance is not a pleasant feeling, so it saps our energy. When I asked for help, my strongest desire was for a solution to get out of my situation. From this starting point all I was sure of was I wanted to be my own boss, which in turn would make me feel happy and free and enable me to be with my baby girl. My desire was intense enough to set the Universe in full motion.

Once you have a desire, the cogs of the Universe start turning to make it happen for you. The results, however, can come quickly or slowly, and I will show you what makes the difference between these two outcomes.

I have outlined above how I didn't know at the time that the result of my desire to change my life would unfold in a series of events that would lead me to this very moment, writing this book. However, since immersing myself in the Law of Attraction and the psychology of goal setting, I have found a way to get results more quickly.

Let me share the evolution of my desires:

1 I sat in the car, cried like a baby and wished I could make some money to stay at home. I had a desire to make £500. (Yep, I was not ambitious at all back then!)

2 A few weeks later, an email came into my inbox titled: 'Want to make an extra £500 a month?' This was one of my first 'aha' moments that this Law of Attraction thing might actually be on to something. I ended up in a programme that taught me how to make me 20 quid here and there, though I quickly saw that that was never going to lead to, let alone fund, my dream life.

3 I started up a wedding dress business at home. I convinced my husband to turn our spare bedroom into a wedding dress boutique and off I went to order a range of dresses from China. I soon realized that most of the people I spoke to had no clue what I was asking of them and I ended up with a somewhat questionable collection of wedding dresses that looked nothing like the pictures. (If you are in the market for a poorly cut, slightly scratchy, off-white wedding dress, I still have one stashed in my attic.) I learned quickly this would not be the business of my dreams and quit.

4 I had to take my sorry ass back to a job that I hated, and to a boss that quite frankly treated me like shit. *C'est la vie.* I needed the money.

5 By happenstance I came across a book on my mum's bookshelf that I felt compelled to read; I discovered coaching and distinctly remember my Soul actively communicating with me via goose bumps. I got that sense of excitement inside me that is usually referred to as a 'gut' feeling. There's more about this later.

6 Having applied to go back to university to become a coach, I fell pregnant with my second daughter. While studying for my postgraduate certificate in coaching, I started to worry again about my financial situation. I would be going on maternity leave and didn't want another nine months of scrimping. So, I put the desire out there for a solution.

7 Another email came through, this one offering advice on how to create a physical product Amazon business.

8 I took a leap of faith as my gut said, 'yes yes yes'. This is an integral part of the process that we will touch on in more detail later.

9 I made my first six figures through the Amazon product business while on my second maternity leave but still didn't feel fulfilled. So, I followed my gut again, as well as the Universal signposts, to start my coaching business. And the rest is history …

As you can see, things happened – not overnight (actually over the course of two years), true, but they did happen. The Universe conspired to help me, and I followed the nudges and took the leaps of faith when I needed to. Those nudges came from my Soul, which I began to trust and listen to despite my Ego contesting the process the whole way. In the meantime, I was also focusing on becoming the best version of myself because I was beginning to understand that the best version of myself could achieve anything. And so I began my spiritual journey … and became a fully fledged publicist for the Universe.

The rules of goal setting

Don't think it, ink it

You need to choose one big goal for each of the eight pathways of life (see the JFDI! task at the end of this chapter). Make a decision. Think about what you truly want and then *write it down*. Written goals are way more potent than those that just float around in the ether. They become concrete and physical. Many studies have shown that people who write down their goals are ten times more likely to achieve them. And the Universe doesn't care if you write in a leather-bound journal with a silver pen or on a tissue with a crayon. All writing is ceremonial and helps you crystallize your desires and gives you a physical object through which to focus your attention.

Honesty is always the best policy

You also need to be brutally honest with yourself about what you want. If you aren't in accurate alignment with the Universe, then your energy will be all over the place. Your desires were given to you for a reason – because they were meant for you. Read that again. If you have a desire, it was *meant* for you. If you are writing down that you want to make £1,000, but, in fact, you desire to attract £1,000,000, then be honest. The Universe knows your deepest desires, so you might as well be honest on paper and dream big, baby.

It needs to feel real

Write goals down that, even though they may be challenging, are possible for you to achieve. If you feel like it's completely impossible, then your energy will scream that, and you won't *ever* get there. If you don't believe you can and will manifest what you desire, then just don't bother. It's as simple as that.

You need to know you can and will do it. There is no room for doubt when it comes to seriously engaging the Universe. Would you doubt that your BFF would be there for you with a box of chocolates and tissues if you broke up with your latest beau/belle? No way. My BFF would always be there. So will the Universe.

If I had set myself a goal to hit £100,000 in the very first month of my business, I wouldn't have been able to formulate a plan of how to get there, and we must always meet the Universe halfway. I wasn't setting myself up for success and, in fact, I would have failed. At that point, I barely had a business at all. When we set goals that feel too far out of our reach and we don't hit them, we lose confidence, and a lack of confidence makes us question our competence. I knew it was possible to make six figures in a month because I had seen others do it, but I didn't believe it was possible for me … yet.

So, I started by setting goals that excited me yet felt achievable, and worked my way up. I then formulated a plan and had my first £100,000 month in Month 10. I had a plan and the Universe came in with bells and whistles and helped me blow my own socks off. I love how it does that, and I want you to know it will do the same for you.

Remember, though: you must formulate a plan to make this happen. A desire will only come to fruition if you put your energy and attention into it and then allow the Universe to do its dance to make it all happen for you. Unfortunately, sitting on your booty scoffing Oreos and watching *Game of Thrones* won't get you to your goals, but a clear plan of action for scaling your business, losing weight or meeting Mr or Ms Right will.

Be specific and state it in the present

The Universe loves juicy details. Specificity allows your attention to be super-focused. If you want a car – what model and make? If you want a boyfriend/girlfriend, what is he/she like? One of the most significant ways in which we hold success away from ourselves is by refusing to nail exactly what we wish to have by when. Because then it's not so scary. And if we fail, we can still dream. Or we can tell ourselves, 'There's always next year.'

So, go back and make sure that you have written dates by all these goals. Give yourself a deadline but don't beat yourself up if you don't hit it. These deadlines aren't tattooed on you, nor will you spontaneously combust if you miss a deadline – it just gives you focus. I had set a goal to get a book deal by December 2017. It didn't happen. Did I give up or berate myself? No way. I trusted the Universe had a more significant plan and made myself another date, another point of focus for my energy, in full faith that one day this book would be in your hand. And guess what? It is.

Goals that are stated in the future create a mental gap for the brain called structural tension. When you state things in the present, this bridges the gap and allows you to believe it's possible. And believing it's possible is precisely the energy you need for manifesting.

So, write your goals down as if they have already happened:

- 'I earn £250k a year.'
- 'I have the most incredible boyfriend/girlfriend who buys me roses every weekend.'
- 'I weigh 9 stone.'
- 'I am in *Guinness World Records* for eating the most doughnuts in one minute.'

I don't care what your goal is, just state it as though it has happened.

Reverse-engineer

This is where you begin to plan out how to achieve your goals. OK, so here is where psychology and spirituality get into a slight conflict and where I am going to help you marry this shizzle up.

The straight-up psychology view would have you make goals that are specific, measurable and thoroughly planned out. Step by step. The spiritual guru would tell you to relax, to trust the Universe and to surrender. I sit in both camps, and this is what I have said to you from the beginning: there is a place for strategy in spirituality and woo-woo in psychology and this is the secret sauce to successful living.

So, I want you to plan, I want your attention to be focused on each step, and I want your attention to have an overall outcome in mind. The best way is to reverse-engineer your goal and work out what the five crucial steps to getting to your goals are. Don't make it any more than five.

I then want you to be dedicated to a process that gets you there, so that you don't slip into the mindset of focusing on the absence of your desire. But here is where the spiritual badass in me pops up and says: 'Follow the plan but know that at any point the Universe may come and slightly divert you or deliver it to you earlier than you expected.'

I had a client who wanted to manifest $300,000 in her business. She planned and planned and executed and didn't make $300,000 in her business but, out of the blue, she inherited $300,000. She got the same result, but via a different route than she initially thought. But because her energy was focused on her own plan, she was in the flow and enjoying herself, and there wasn't time to worry about where that $300,000 was coming from. She just had faith that it was coming.

The F-word

Once you are clear about your goals, we need to add in a special ingredient that is integral to your success. Let me be clear here: if you look at the list of goals you have written and you don't believe it's possible, then you are missing a vital ingredient in ticking off your goal list one by one. In the words of the late great George Michael, 'You gotta have faith, faith, faith'. In the JFDI! exercise, I will get you to split each goal into steps and then get you tick off each step. Goals seem big and scary because instead of looking at the next step, you end up focusing on the huge big picture, which your brain cannot compute. As you achieve each step, you build up your faith muscle, and you have the confidence to go to the next stage. Sometimes, faith needs to be your downpayment on your future.

Have faith in your power to manifest anything you want, and it will come to you. You must believe in yourself and the Universe. You must feel this is yours and you deserve it. Otherwise, you won't get it. All you have to do is decide, set an intention, and have a plan, as well as keep faith and have belief. Take steps your end but allow the Universe to take care of the rest.

Check that all your goals are in alignment with your personal vision for your life and getting you to the overall desired outcome for your life. Strengthening your faith muscle is paramount and you will get little signs from the Universe that you are on course if you keep your eye out.

Make a note if you see things related to your goal showing up in your life. I call it my evidence list because it's proof that the Universe is working on my behalf.

Have fun, babycakes!

Remember to set goals that you can enjoy attaining – we need to attach positive emotion to the process. Why? Because then you can be sure that you are tuning in to UniverseFM and this will get you there so much more quickly. When you are having fun and giving attention to your intention (desire), the Universe will orchestrate an infinite number of events to materialize your desires. It always has your back; it is your BFF, remember! Intention and attention are two partners-in-crime when it comes to you manifesting.

But there is a caveat that a lot of 'manifesters' get wrong. Your goal may be for the future, but your attention and energy must stay in the present. If you are continually thinking about the absence of the thing you are trying to manifest, your energy has now shifted, and in fact you are pushing what you want further away. That is why we need to learn to be super-duper conscious.

Expect the unexpected

Sometimes the Universe will deliver something slightly different from what you originally wanted. Sometimes you will wonder why the outcome was different, but you need to trust that, if you follow the steps in the book, clean up your energy and raise your vibe, the Universe will deliver only great things. It might be a slightly different outcome, but it will be one that is better than your conditioned mind initially conceived.

It also means you need to be *open* to the opportunity and *detached* from the outcome. You still have the intention of going in a particular direction (your goal). However, between point A and point B, there are infinite possibilities. When you factor in uncertainty, you embrace the reality that things might change direction at any given moment if you find something more exciting.

So being specific allows you to focus your attention but also to embrace the flexibility that the Universe may surprise you with something even more amazeballs.

EMMA'S STORY

Emma focuses all her energy into creating a successful business, and she is making more money than she ever has. The problem is, she can't enjoy it because her husband is constantly arguing with her, complaining that he barely sees her. Because her husband is continually arguing with her, Emma seeks solace in eating chocolate every day and her weight creeps up, and now she looks in the mirror and feels rubbish. Whenever her friends ask her to go out with them, she makes excuses as she thinks she looks fat in everything. Because she is stuck in the house, she feels frustrated and takes this out on her kids.

There are eight areas you must focus on in order to create balanced success in your life. So many people put all their energy into bettering one part of their life and neglect other parts. This is why I wholeheartedly believe so many people feel unfulfilled.

When I focused and committed to improving my life across the board, the real magic started to happen. I was so busy and involved in creating the best version of me that I had no attention left to worry about, or compare myself to, anybody around me.

HARRY'S STORY

Harry has got a promotion in his job, but this means lots of travel and his eating habits and health have taken a back seat. He used to volunteer at his local church, which gave him a sense of fulfilment, but he is so tired now that all he wants to do at the weekend is sit on the sofa and watch Netflix. He has wanted to meet Ms Right for ages, but his energy is low because of the bad eating habits and his social life is suffering.

CLAIRE'S STORY

Claire is a total social butterfly. She loves to party and has lots of friends, but she feels lost career-wise. She spends most of her time hungover and goes to her job on autopilot but ends up spending her money on designer clothes, so she's ready for her next night out. She has no savings and deep down she wants to leave her job and start her own business, but she doesn't know how to and is worried that if she doesn't have the money from her career, she will lose her social life which is the only thing that makes her happy (or so she thinks). After all her spending, she can't afford to join a gym, so she doesn't get much exercise.

As you can see from these stories, all parts of our lives are inextricably linked and have an impact on one another. That's why to get real happiness all round, we must set badass goals in all areas of our life and commit to balanced growth.

Ready for the next steps, darling?

Once you have a clear idea of the goals you wish to set in each area of your life, you also have clarity on your direction and know what you desire, which is the fuel that you need to take action.

- Execute the plan you have.
- Take action and *trust* the Universe to handle the details.

Remember that the Universe gives you both the soil and the seed (energy and information), but it's up to you to carry out the daily task of working in the fields (attention) as well as keeping the faith (intention) that one day the seed will grow into that juicy, ripe, red tomato (the manifestation of your desires). Trust that, when things don't seem to go your way, there is a reason that is beyond your understanding. There is always a time and a place to channel your inner Elsa and just 'Let It Go'.

Do exactly what you would do if you were getting it today, and take actions in your life to reflect that strong expectation and desire. You need to make room for your wishes to come in, and understand that expectation is a truly powerful force. We will delve into this in more detail later.

TOP TAKEAWAYS

- To get success in your life, you need to know where you are going.
- Even if you don't see the *exact* route, just know how you want to feel. Get clarity on your ideal life and what that looks like.
- Write down goals in all eight areas of your life. When your focus is on becoming the best version of yourself, getting what you desire will be a million times easier. Remember that if it isn't written down, it's fantasy.
- Plan, plan, plan. Yet still accept that the plan may change.
- Implement a daily goal-setting routine. This is where the magic happens.

JFDI!

Balance those badass goals

There are eight areas of life for which you should make goals. When you focus on all these areas and build up goals over the year, this has a compound effect on your whole life. If you could improve in all areas of your life, even just little by little, month on month, by the end of the year your life would look drastically different.

The areas are:

- Spiritual (your connection to the Universe/God … whatever or whomever)
- Emotional (your relationship to your closest family members/partner/children)
- Physical (your physical health)
- Mental (your learning and mental growth)
- Social (your friendships and community)
- Charitable (how you give to others outside of yourself)
- Vocational (what you do for a living)
- Financial (your relationship to money and how you build your wealth).

Set yourself 12-month goals in each of the areas. Then reverse-engineer the goals and break them down into *no more than five* key steps. You may have multiple goals but try not to have more than three in each area, otherwise it becomes overwhelming. The reason we focus on all areas of your life is to maintain balance.

While life would feel really amazing even if you achieved success in one or two areas of your life, think about how incredible it would be if you improved in all the areas listed above. How would it feel to look back over a year to find that your health, wealth, relationships and vocation had all improved: it would be *epic*, right?!

Download an expanded version of this goal-setting exercise at www.noorhibbert.com/book.

4

Goodbye, Comparison Hangover

Become so engulfed in creating your own success that you don't even care what others are doing.

I'm excited that you have taken the time to really start looking at your big goals and what you envision for your life. Now
you have to actually make it happen. In order to go for big
hairy scary goals, you need to become totally aware of where
you have come from, what's been driving you and what is not
serving you. It's time to militantly create the best version of
you, spiritually, emotionally and mentally, so that you can just
fucking go for it.

I had a wonderful lady come to work with me and she said
to me that I represented everything she didn't believe in, but
also realized that, after 43 years of doing things 'her way' and not
really achieving the level of fulfilment she desired, it was time
for a change. It takes balls to admit that your life isn't the pretty,
perfect picture that you have so diligently tried to portray on
social media, and even bigger balls to decide to change it.

I understood where she was coming from because, a few
years earlier, that was exactly the spot I had been in and it
was the journey of awareness that unpeeled me and helped
me build myself up again. I am merely hypothesizing that you
don't feel full of all that life has to offer and you keep looking
at every body else's perfectly filtered Instagram feeds wondering how they have got their shit together. You may spend hours
pondering why you aren't making as much money in your life,
or going from one unhappy relationship to another, or spending way too much time in a never-ending battle with your
body, when everyone on social media is seemingly busy doing
the exact opposite and sharing it for all the world to see –
#selfie. Whether it's one of those things or all of them, I hear
you, I see you and I have got you.

The comparison conspiracy

I want to let you in on something that I have come to realize:
I don't actually think it was curiosity that killed the cat. I'll tell

you what I think the real story is. One day, a most beautiful cat was born into the world. Happy, carefree and full of joy, she was destined to be one badass pussy. Then one day she started to see the other cats, with different coloured coats, some better at chasing mice and some getting more affection from their owners. Then it happened, the moment that would change that cat's path in life for ever, the first time she asked herself: 'What is wrong with me?' She carried the burden of not matching up to the other cats, which led to some feline depression and she got so tired of trying to live up to everyone else's perfect life that she gave up. You see, my dear, it wasn't curiosity but comparison that killed the cat.

I want you to think about the times that you have tried to get ahead, be better than everyone else, come first, get the best grades, get to the best university, work for the biggest company, drive the flashiest car, buy the biggest house or get the most love.

Who were you competing against? Who was setting your expectations? Where in life are you saying, 'She's better than me' or 'How did he get ahead so quickly?' or 'Why is she so much prettier, skinnier?' Perhaps you catch yourself comparing your marriage, your children, your business or your body with other people's. Where in life are you failing to see opportunities for your own personal growth because you are so wrapped up in the successes of everyone else?

It seems pretty crazy that we would go through life living up, or down, to other people's expectations but that is exactly what we are conditioned to do from the moment we make our way down the birth canal to the sound of gentle breathing, or, in the case of my first two kids, a barrage of expletives. (I was as cool as a cucumber when my third came along as I birthed her on my sofa, but that's another story.)

When we are babies, we aren't busy looking at other babies thinking 'Oh shit, that dude has started walking – I am a total and utter failure.' These imaginary yardsticks which we unconsciously use for comparing ourselves are actually imposed on us by our parents, teachers and society at large as we grow up. At school, it's a race to see who's cleverest, who's the sportiest or who will get the lead role in the end-of-year play. As we grow older, at work it's who will be the boss's favourite, who will get the promotion, and who will get the cheeky snog at the Christmas party from the new hottie in the office.

Unwittingly we get lobbed on to life's comparison conveyor belt and it just keeps us going round and round, making us feel dizzy with the constant feeling that we aren't good enough or where we should be for where we are in life. This creates the sinking feeling of never reaching that elusive destination where everything is just going to be 'just perfect'. This feeling leaves your energy in a funk that is totally not conducive to success or manifesting. The reality is that, in every part of our lives, there is an opportunity to feel as though we have failed. And when this starts to mount up over time we are left with a totally false, yet deep-rooted, belief system about who we are at the core that then determines how we carry on in the future. That's why in the previous chapter I asked you to focus on what you really want in your life, not what you *think* you want because everyone else has it.

It was the winter of 2005 and I was about to head out to the student union for another night of alcohol-fuelled debauchery with my best friends, but as I looked at them dressing their perfectly formed size-6 figures in their gorgeous body-con dresses and applying make-up to their perfectly clear skin, a familiar feeling came over me. As I scanned my curvy physique and vigilantly applied a 3-inch-thick layer of foundation to my face, to cover the new cluster of spots that had appeared, I felt anger, envy and sadness. I felt fat and unattractive, and it just wasn't fair. I remember so clearly that I threw myself on to the floor in a heap of tears and felt physically sick, and even then

I scorned myself for being such a mess. The thing was, I wasn't overweight but, in *comparison* with my friends, I felt huge.

When you go through life like this, you are setting yourself up for failure instead of success because, if you are always looking out for how others are doing better, looking better, being better, then you will always find this to be the case. In psychology, this is called confirmation bias. And for those suffering with low self-esteem, every time we make comparisons it feeds that pesky Ego with more ammo and it will chitter chatter until all that negative self-talk leads us on a downward spiral into depression. The thing I didn't realize back then in my early twenties was that I had a choice to change everything I didn't like about myself. But I was so sucked up in my own victim mentality that I couldn't see the possibility or opportunity for my own growth. Instead, I just drowned my sorrows in shots of cheap tequila which I would proceed to vomit up the next morning. Sexy.

From a psychological perspective, it has been said that we make comparisons as a way of evaluating ourselves, which in turn enables our brain to develop an understanding of who we are, what we are good at and what we suck at. This happens both consciously and unconsciously. Then there is the ever-growing world of social media, which just acts like kerosene being poured on to the flame of comparison. Social media has massively increased the information about people that we're exposed to and forces our minds to assess it on the train to work, when we are going for a wee or lying in bed at 2 a.m. Instead of just looking at our BFFs for comparison, we now have the whole world to compare ourselves to and it's all too easy to contrast our day-to-day reality to the touched-up, Photoshopped, sepia-filtered fragments of someone else's.

The problem is, as human beings, we look around at what is happening outside before deciding how to feel on the inside, and this is something I want you to become aware of and start changing as it will free you from the grasp of comparison that has been weighing you down and stopping you from living the life you have been dreaming of. When you are scrolling down your newsfeed and subjected to a barrage of images that serve only as a reminder of where you aren't, this just creates more negativity in your mind. It amplifies fears, pressures and insecurities by showing you the 'highlights reel' of other people's lives.

When you are constantly comparing yourself to others, how can you ever really know what you want or be truly happy with what you have got? If you are on a perpetual quest to keep up with the Joneses, the Smiths and the Kardashians, you deny yourself the very gift of tapping into the power of finding your true purpose and living a life that makes you happy. In addition, if you are fixated on what other people have, you may be cajoled into thinking that *that* it is what you want.

So how would it feel to face the other way?

How about taking your gaze from the outside world and start looking inward at your Soul? It is there to guide you every step of the way towards the exact destination you have set out to get to. However, in order to hear it, you need to quieten the noise. Wouldn't it be utterly liberating to be able to ignore the successes or failures of others in an attempt to focus wholly on you: to learn more, to love more and to grow more into the most epic version of yourself?

What would it be like to totally own your life in all its glory and focus on you becoming the best version of you instead of a best version of you compared to everyone around you? When you do this, you are tapping into the power of your own pure potential that is lying at your very core but hasn't yet been used. Focusing on everybody else drains your energy, which then leaves you in a manifesting funk. When you become obsessed with your own personal growth rather than your personal growth in relation to others, you will unlock magic in your life and your manifesting power will be unleashed. Become so engulfed in creating your own success that you don't even care what others are doing.

Of course, measuring yourself against others is a modus operandi of the human mind, and in some ways it can actually be helpful, if we can control our thoughts. The inspiration you get from someone else's achievements can push you to improve your own life. I know that when I've seen someone flaunting their peachy booty in the gym, it makes me more motivated to go and achieve the same. How would it feel to be inspired by others' successes and to know that if it's possible for them then it's possible for you, too?

I made a conscious choice to become totally aware of my feelings when comparing myself to others. When I felt that little green-eyed monster popping up devilishly at my shoulder, I used that feeling to push me to do better. I came to realize that, if I felt envy when looking at others, it meant that I desired that thing. Whether it was pictures of toned abs, a Piña Colada beach shot or a happy couple, I embraced the fact that these were my desires and I set out to get them. I truly believe that if a desire is put inside us it is meant for us. Use your envy as a catalyst for personal growth.

It's time to screw the scoreboard.

When social media stirs up feelings of inadequacy, there are some pretty obvious ways to get rid of the funk. You can go totally cold turkey (yep, I said it) as you embark on your journey of self-discovery and awesomeness and delete apps or even deactivate accounts. You could ruthlessly prune your lists of friends and get rid of those who stir up negative feelings in you, while you work on your inner self until you are in a position where you just don't give a shit any more.

Ultimately, the greatest protection against the dreaded comparison hangover – and the best way to pull yourself out of it – is to develop and maintain a stable sense of self. That means focusing on growing your identity and self-esteem, giving energy to a select posse of peeps who get the real you, and staying aligned to your beliefs and values. Basically, it's owning your shit and being proud of the person you are in real life, not the person you curate for Instagram.

The comparison hangover clinic

So, the Australians are a pretty ingenious people. I found out recently on a trip to Sydney that they have hangover clinics. You rock up feeling like you want to die because your brain has been turned into mashed potato by an eclectic mix of spirits. They hook you up to a drip and 30 minutes later – voilà – you are a new person. Well, I want you to imagine that it's time for you to get hooked up to the comparison detox drip.

The first step to manifesting all that you desire in your life is to *get rid* of the belief that you are in any sort of competition with the outside world. Instead, start looking inward to your Soul and the guidance it offers. When you look outward for validation, acceptance or reward, you are giving away your power. Hold on to your power by deciding that from *today* you will own your journey and your life and make the wholehearted choice to set your own expectations instead of living up to those that have been forced upon you all your life so far. Make the bold decision that you will no longer allow yourself to feel the pain of someone else's progress by comparing it to yours.

As soon as you do this, all feelings of envy, fear, anxiety and anger will start to dissipate. It becomes all about you and your inner journey. You will start to align with the Universe and attract people on the same journey as you, and because of this you will start to celebrate and be inspired by other people's successes. As you change your inner world, the outer world around you will change. As you grow into a better version of yourself, you will start to manifest the most incredible things in the world.

I want you to decide that your successes and failures are yours alone to learn from and that they do not reflect your self-worth. Decide that you are no longer defined by what you own and what you have achieved but *by who you are at the very core* – an amazing human with all the potential to create whatever you desire. Know that as long as you are improving every day in every area of your life that you are exactly where you need to be. If you haven't done the JFDI! task in Chapter 3 go back and do it now. This will lay the foundation for you to be super-focused on you.

An amazing way to allow that comparison hangover drip to work its magic gradually is by counting your blessings every day and practising deep gratitude for where you are in your life and what is good in your own life. Happy people use themselves for an internal evaluation, and I want you to start doing this. Instead of comparing yourself with others, simply compare yourself with previous versions of yourself. Looking at where you have come from in relation to you and only you is far more empowering.

TOP TAKEAWAYS

- Comparison killed the cat, not curiosity.
- When you are wrapped up in the successes of everyone else, you fail to see opportunities for your own personal growth.
- Instead of looking outward for validation, look inward.
- If looking at social media takes you down a rabbit hole of comparison, quit the looking.
- Your journey is yours alone – only seek to be better than you were yesterday.

JFDI!

Fuck the failure

This task is to figure out who is setting your yardsticks and where you are suffering from a comparison hangover.

Consider for a moment all the areas of life in which you feel like you have 'failed' right now or could be doing better.

- Could you or should you be in better shape?
- Could you or should you have more love in your life?
- Could or should your finances be better than they are?
- Could you or should you have better friendships in your life?
- Could or should your business be doing better than it is?
- Could you or should you be serving the world in a better way?

Of these, note down on a piece of paper your top three perceived failures.

Now you have a list of three things that you judge yourself to have failed at.

Next, I want you to stop and consider against whose yardstick you have failed by. Dig deep and truly understand who or what has been your puppet master until now.

- Is it magazines and television shows?
- Is it your parents or siblings?
- Is it your friends?

How have you actually come to the conclusion that where you are is a sign of having failed rather than just the place in life where you need to be right now, so you can move onwards to the next phase?

Who decided that your current state of progress is a failure?

Now look back at where you have come from:

- Where did you start?
- How have you already grown to be the amazing human being you are today?

Think about the opportunities for growth that the failure presents you with right now and the future benefits that this growth will have on your life.

Let your new mantra be:

I am exactly where I need to be, and I know exactly where to go.
This is my journey and I will love it fully.

5

Say Boo to the Bullshit

In order to move forward courageously in life, you need to figure out what thoughts have been holding you back.

Let's play hide and seek. But in this version we need to find the stories that you have been telling yourself (consciously and unconsciously) on repeat, that are stopping you from really going for your goals. If you have been trying to change something in your life and, for some reason, you keep struggling to actually make the change, there will be an internal narrative getting in the way.

Like pesky weeds that overtake your garden of potential awesomeness, your limiting beliefs must be dug out and you need to turn your attention to any non-serving stories that may be getting in the way of your fulfilling your desires. Then, like my favourite card game, we are going to shout 'BULLSHIT!' at all of it. Not bullshit for it happening, but bullshit to it still holding you back from your greatness. Can I hear a hallelujah?

When you find out what is lurking below your conscious thoughts and also embrace the unprocessed shame, guilt, resentment and so on, you open yourself up to an inspiring future. Old stories that are not conducive to success that began forming in childhood create resistance to achieving what you want.

Even though you may consciously really want something, just below the surface of that desire are probably beliefs and emotions that are in total conflict with your dream. In order to move forward courageously in life, you need to figure out what thoughts have been holding you back. You need to whip out one big almighty shovel and start digging. Take a deep breath: we are going to go deep.

The truth is, the only obstacles between you and the life you desire, are your thoughts. Up until this point in your life, you have been 'automatically created' and the automatic programming that created you most likely wasn't configured to create the best version of you. The automatic creation of you has happened without your awareness, as a result of conditioning, modelling and feelings that you have attached to the experiences you have gone through. Your thoughts don't belong to you. You may think them, but that's because your brain is just processing all the data and pulling out what it feels is relevant. You are just the thinker of the thoughts, but the thoughts are not you. However, your thoughts determine how you feel, and feelings power your actions.

Feelings take precedence over logic. Your memories and beliefs about certain situations cause strong feelings that drive every action you take. You need to shift into manual gear and take control. It's your awareness of the negative stories you have made up about yourself, and of how they may have been holding you back, that sets you free and puts you back in the driver's seat of your own life.

Isn't using the Law of Attraction enough?

Maybe you are questioning that, if the Universe is as powerful as I say, then surely some positive thinking and a vision board is enough. The answer is no. If it was yes, then this book would not be bringing in psychology, too. You can't sit all day saying affirmations, making goals, spending hours carefully cutting out photos of pristine beaches and sports cars to stick on to your vision board, if the stories that you are telling yourself are in *conflict* with your desires. This is a sure-fire way to end up in manifesting limbo.

If you want to manifest the dream relationship but you have created a powerful story deep down (at an identity level) that you don't deserve love (because, say, you never received love from your dad as a child), then you can meditate on your vision board all you like and yet still struggle to find Mr/Ms Right. This is because deep down you don't really believe that you are worthy of love and so unconsciously you will be giving off that energy to the Universe. Daddy issues are a real thing, people!

If you are trying to build a million-dollar business and have a vision board adorned with dollar bills and yet deep down you hold a story that being rich would make you a douche bag, then you will sabotage your business goals on a subconscious level. Our brains are designed to keep us safe, and since one of our biggest human drivers is love and security, anything that would jeopardize that will cause us to sabotage ourselves.

So, it's imperative that you understand that the Law of Attraction picks up on the negative vibes that your stories hold, which then *block* the positive outcome you are trying to achieve. To unblock those outcomes, therefore, you have to uncover the bullshit stories, change the energy and truly believe that you can achieve what you want. Your stories and your goals need to be aligned. Capiche?

So, in order to ensure that our energy is totally aligned with co-creating with the Universe, we need to find out what those stories are. Once we call 'bullshit' on them, they cannot work so powerfully in our subconscious. The awareness weakens the stronghold of the stories, which then makes way for you to be totally energetically vibing with your goals with no hidden agendas lurking below the surface

Time to be a Soul digger

There are a few steps that you need to take in order to pull those weeds out. I like to call this Soul digging, and it's the process required to uncover your most powerful self. The steps are:

1 Understand what your stories are.
2 Acknowledge where they came from.
3 Call bullshit on them.
4 Change your bullshit stories.
5 Create a new self-identity that matches up to the new stories that you will create.

For the purpose of exploring these ideas, I'm going to use money and the beliefs around money – our 'money stories' – as my primary example. There are also body stories, relationship stories and family stories, but today we will focus on money. Though people may tell you that money doesn't bring you happiness, it does bring freedom and, if used in the right way, can be utilized as a vehicle for happiness. When you look at your goals list, for most of them, I'm going to bet, money is required.

Growing up in a religious household, my dad had strong beliefs about money. He always drummed it into us about giving to charity and he had even stronger views about the 'corrupt rich'. Even to this day, he makes comments about rich people being greedy. What I didn't realize is that I began to believe him.

My mind put 2 + 2 together and created the story in my head that being rich would make me greedy. Since my dad (who I love very much) hates rich greedy people, so the story inside me told me that, if I created wealth, my dad would hate me. Therefore, not being rich was actually a safer option in that it would keep me being loved. As I explained above, as humans, our biggest driver is love. We all just want to be loved and safe. And if anything jeopardizes that, we will stop it. For me, becoming rich could jeopardize that. As you can see 2 + 2 here actually equals being poor.

JESSICA'S STORY

Jessica saw her dad work 24/7 and, although he was successful and wealthy, he was miserable. Her story was that wealth equals stress and so she kept herself broke because wealth clearly did not equal happiness.

EMMA'S STORY

Emma saw her mother working hard in her own business and that meant Emma and her siblings were looked after by nannies. Emma wanted to be a mother and when she became one she found herself financially struggling. We uncovered that she had a deep-rooted belief that, if she was successful, she would neglect her children. So, she kept herself broke so she could be a good mother.

AARON'S STORY

Aaron kept hitting an income ceiling in his business, and it transpired that, as he had become more successful, he felt compelled to keep giving money to his friends and family, because he felt guilty for having it. As we delved into his particular money story, he realized that his dad had always done the exact same thing as he had come from a poor background and had strong family values when it came to financially supporting those you loved. Aaron took on these beliefs and started to act in the same way, even though it wasn't a conscious decision.

As you can see from the above examples, our money stories are powerful and also irrational.

You will also see that money stories are mostly learned from our darling parents and those closest to us as we grew up, and for the most part they are created and embedded in our psyche as children. All of us have some skewed equation in our minds that stops us from becoming rich. Sometimes, it's easier to tell ourselves that 'being rich' would make us evil, so then we don't make the effort to start a new business that could fulfil us on a deeper level. Therefore, our negative stories serve a purpose of keeping us 'safe', even if they are suffocating us and keeping us from our true potential.

The reality is, however, that money is neutral. It is just a kind of energy, which is why it is referred to as currency. In one sense, it doesn't really exist. The paper you hold in your hand that represents a £5 or £10 or £50 note is just a value that the piece of paper represents. The actual paper is worthless. It's the value that we attach to it that's important. When you log on to an online banking site, you are just looking at numbers on a screen, yet the numbers have the power to induce fear and anxiety or, conversely, happiness. All these reactions are a result of what you think and believe about money, which is why it's important you get up close and personal with your own money story.

Let's start digging

So here is a task for you. I want you to grab a pen and flip to the note section at the end of this book. I want you to write out your ideal yearly income. Once you have done that, I want you to look at the paper, take your pen and add a zero to the end of it.

Have you done that?

Now, look at the second figure. If I told you now that you had to earn that amount *this* year, what comes up for you? What do you feel and think as you look at that number?

Write everything down on that same page. Anything and everything, however stupid or small.

Now you have in front of you the set of beliefs you have formed, and this is a great starting point for unearthing your money stories. These stories have been producing fake limits on your earning potential, and it's time to figure out where those pesky beliefs came from.

You need to shoot the messenger

I don't care who made up the saying that told us not to, but I'm telling you now: it's time to shoot the messenger. You need to find out where your beliefs come from and then, meta-phorically of course, shoot the person who gave them to you. The reason is that that story does not *belong to you*. It belonged to someone else and they kindly gave it to you and now it's messing up your manifesting mojo. As soon as you recognize that you were not brought into this world with that story, you can begin the process of letting it go.

Perhaps, in the task above, you wrote down things like:

- 'I am not clever enough to make that money.'
- 'I don't have a clue how to make that money.'
- 'I don't want or need that money.'

Go one step deeper: question all the reasons why you couldn't go and make that money with the extra zero. Perhaps you think that your family would judge you, or your friends would want you to give it to them or that you would be scared of all the extra taxes. The reason why finding these things out is so important is because it's those stories that are currently defining your actions when it comes to making the moolah. And it's believing those stories that are keeping so many people broke, when they have the potential to be truly abundant.

Whether it's money, relationships or food, there are always some clues in your earliest memories as to where your negative stories come from. If my clients tell me they aren't clever enough to make money or not pretty enough for someone to love them, I always ask them to think back to a time before the age of 12 when they first felt that feeling. This is usually a great indication of where these irrational stories originated.

I want you to think back to when you were little. What did you hear about money? Did your parents tell you money didn't grow on trees? Or did you hear the phrase 'We are comfortable' all the time? By recognizing the language you were surrounded with regarding the subject of money, you can begin to unravel why you believe certain things. Perhaps you bought into the whole 'rich people are evil' story, like I did. (We will talk more about the power of the language you use in Chapter 8.)

Here is a list of negative beliefs about being rich you may be holding:

- Being rich is evil.
- Rich people don't have friends.
- Being rich will make you stressed.
- In order to become wealthy, you must sacrifice family time.
- Being rich will mean paying more tax.

You get my drift.

Money mistakes you have made

The next powerful thing to do is recognize the past mistakes you have made around money. Maybe you have got badly into debt once or have been declared bankrupt. Perhaps you got into a financial dispute with a partner or lost money in a bad investment. Maybe you are terrible at saving or spend all your money irresponsibly.

These experiences have negative energy attached to them and are also stopping you from finding the financial success you deserve. As long as you personalize your lack of money, you will not make money. When you recognize the mistakes you have made about money and your ruthless, unforgiving self-talk around that, you can really start to move forward.

Write down all the things that you are bad at when it comes to money. Any bad experiences that come to mind, however big or small.

I know we have focused on money in this chapter, but you can use the same process to uncover your stories around relationships. A great starting place for this is looking at the nature of your parents' relationship. Look back, too, at your own earliest relationships.

Breathe out the bullshit

Clearing out your money blocks or any other blocks and stories can be a painful experience, and, quite honestly, lots of people would rather just go on day to day, paying bills and plodding on, without really reaching their full potential. Money is just energy and it flows to whoever wants it. But in order to want it, you need to have carried out the excavation of your limiting beliefs I've described above,

By now, I hope, you should have uncovered some of your limiting money beliefs, recognized where they have come from and be ready to do some work on changing them. One simple yet effective task is to write down all those beliefs on a piece of paper. Go through each one and write next to it the total opposite in relation to you.

For example, if you think rich people are evil, write down: 'I am rich, and I give generously to all.' If you have the belief that building a business makes you stressed, write down the oppo-site: 'I am building a successful business with ease and flow.'

TOP TAKEAWAYS
. . . .

- Just below the surface of every desire is probably a bullshit story that is in conflict with that desire, and subconsciously stopping you.
- You are the thinker of these stories, but these stories do not belong to you. They are just data being pushed out of your brain.
- We have created internal beliefs about money, relationships and our body, all mostly stemming from childhood.
- You need to be aware of what these limiting beliefs are by doing some soul digging. This will weaken their hold on you.
- Shoot the messenger and detach yourself from these stories so you can move towards your dreams with gusto.

JFDI!

Tap, tap, tap: the Emotional Freedom Technique

One of the most powerful ways to energetically change your feelings and beliefs around money is through a technique called tapping, aka the Emotional Freedom Technique (EFT). EFT is defined and described as a clinical procedure for the relief of psychological and physical distress. It's a process of removing the negative emotional charge of negative stories, so that they no longer affect you. Tapping combines the cognitive reprocessing benefits of exposure and acceptance therapy with the energetic disturbance releases associated with acupuncture and other energy therapies.

The cause of all negative emotions and beliefs is a disturbance in our body's energy system. The energy system is the same system that is used in acupuncture. Acupuncture posits that there are pathways in our bodies called energy meridians. All of our negative emotions, such as anxiety, anger, shame, guilt, hurt and so on, are due to a disturbance in one or more of these energy meridians. These energy disturbances are connected to memories of painful events. When we think of the memory, the associated energy disturbance gets activated, which then causes the negative and sometimes even painful emotions.

EFT works by intentionally and powerfully activating an energy disturbance as you think about a negative memory or just 'feel your feelings'. While the energy disturbance is activated, you tap with your fingertips on the meridian points in order to clear out the energy disturbance in the affected areas.

As the disturbance gets cleared through the tapping, you will feel your negative emotions actually start to disappear. When the energy disturbance has been completely cleared, your negative emotions will have gone. You can then think about the memory with no nasty emotional reaction! Then you tap in new positive affirmations and emotions. It's like pulling out weeds and planting sunflowers.

Head to www.noorhibbert.com/book and follow the tapping tutorial so that you can use tapping to help you reprogram your mind for success.

Once we start clearing out the old negative stories and emotions, we can start crafting a new self-identity that is stronger happier and more determined to go out there and do big things in the world. We are going to delve deeper into creating a new self-identity in the next chapter that is really going to help you to create your most abundant life.

6

It's Time for a Spiritual Facelift

When you can peel back the layers, you will find someone truly spectacular who really believes in themselves — someone unique, who has talents and a big fat purpose on this planet.

I had dreamed my whole childhood of parading on a Hollywood set or dancing in a Broadway show. The fact I couldn't act or sing very well was a minor technicality but what was more worrying was the resounding noise from the adults in my life that such ambitions were unrealistic, and I would forever need a backup plan. My imagination and capacity to daydream was quashed and I was slowly moulded into a girl who believed those kinds of things were not possible.

I played by the rules and did what I needed to do, but then felt even more confused because nothing ever felt *right*. I was a round peg surrounded by a bazillion square holes. Do you know that feeling? I thought that there must be something wrong with me because when I looked at everyone around me they seemed to be getting jobs with fancy titles and getting all the usual trappings of a successful career.

What the heck was I meant to be doing in my life? Or, going deeper, what was the point of life?

When we are born into this magical place called the world as joyful little babies, we are full of potential for taking centre stage in our life. We all have the capacity to do something awesome and we are right on track to do it … until … well, life happens.

Parents happen, school happens, society happens and, as I've explained, we get lost in an abyss of conditioning and end up being someone or doing something because we feel we have to or because we have learned to be that way. Since you are now aware of what comparing yourself has done for you (see Chapter 4) and you are now making a serious commitment to focus on you, I need you to figure out who the hell you are. I want to strip you down and find out who you really are underneath, wobbly bits and all …

- *Not* who you have had to be in your family
- *Not* who you have had to be at work
- *Not* who you have had to be to please your partner.

Who are you?

I want you to recognize where along the way you have been moulded into someone you perhaps don't want to be. Because if you base how you live your life on how everyone expects you to, you literally give all your power over to other people and become debilitatingly dependent on someone outside of yourself for validation.

When you can peel back the layers, you will find someone truly spectacular who really believes in themselves – someone unique, who has talents and a big fat purpose on this planet. When you uncover that purpose and what lights you up, it's like snorting unicorn crack and you get this divine buzz of happiness. It's the best legal high going.

However, uncovering who you really are takes some Soul-digging, and setting the goals that you truly want to achieve is the first step. This is your first indication of who you really are and what is important to you. Then you can rewrite the conditioning by making the conscious choice to choose who you want to be.

That was one of the most powerful things that anyone ever told me – that I could choose to be who I wanted to be; that I had a choice to drop the need to be what my parents expected, my school wanted, and society pushed for. I could say goodbye to the self-imposed labels of 'depressed', 'anxious', 'envious' or 'unsuccessful' and choose a new identity that was empowering.

Because underneath it all the real you is so powerful. I want you to understand that who you are at the very core is the most powerful version of you. Who you are at the very core isn't bothered about comparing yourself with others, isn't worried about failing, and unequivocally knows that you can create the life you daydream about.

Just for a moment, imagine what our world would be like if everyone was happy to be themselves and shamelessly loved themselves so much that they weren't bothered by the opinions of others, the colour of their skin, how educated they were or whether they were a man one day or a woman the next. We should all be allowed to be whoever the hell we want to be unapologetically.

I want you to choose who *you want to be* and own it like a boss.

The psychology

Your present self-image – the idea you have of your abilities, appearance and personality – was created by your own imagination from pictures of yourself; pictures built up from interpretations and evaluations that you placed on your experiences. You may remember, from Chapter 1, that when I was four years old a girl walked up to me in the playground and quizzed me about the bushiness of my eyebrows. Ugh. Under the age of seven, what we hear, we believe to be fact. I interpreted that experience in my little head and came to the conclusion that I was different and ugly. This became the self-image I held about myself for two long decades.

In addition, you also learn what to believe and how to behave from those closest to you through a process called 'modelling'. If your mum constantly nags your father, and you father always puts up with it, it will be likely that you will adopt that way of operating around your future partners. This happens on a subconscious level and is why we are so similar to one or both of our parents. We become conditioned to behave in a certain way. All this comes about because of the totally erroneous idea that 'I should be like everybody else'.

So, as you can see, it is all the events and experiences throughout your life that have created layers of smog around the most empowered version of you that lies at your core. The way that you see yourself is absolutely crucial to the life you manifest. Your self-image will dictate all your thoughts, which in turn will create your feelings, actions and behaviours. It also affects your abilities.

However, if your self-image hasn't been helping you reach the success you want, then you will be thrilled to know that you can change it. Your past identity, which has brought you to where you are today, does not and will not be the identity that takes you to the new phase of your rock star life.

In the same way that you have created an identity that has got you to where you are today, you will create an even better one to get you to where you want to be next month, next year or a decade away. Numerous studies have shown that anybody, young or old, can alter the ways they not only see themselves but also how they act and consequently their life. BOOM!

One of the reasons we humans think it is so hard to reshape ourselves is because it has taken us decades to become the person we are today, so it is clearly no easy feat to redesign ourselves all over again. When you become habituated to one way of doing and being, everything becomes so deeply engrained that you believe it's all unchangeable. You will strongly hold on to your beliefs even if they are sabotaging your success. Henry Ford so wisely said: 'The man who thinks he can and the man who thinks he can't are both right'. So which camp are you in? If you don't believe you can achieve it, whatever it is, there is absolutely no chance that you will.

Let me be crystal clear: changing your self-image isn't just about repeating 'positive words' and hoping that, in a puff of smoke, you will magically turn from a frog into a prince or princess. You cannot just sprinkle unicorn glitter on to a pile of shit and expect that pile of shit to smell or look any better. Changing how you see yourself is deep work and requires a good clean out of the crap first. It is also impossible to think positively if your self-image is negative at its core.

Your beliefs about who you are shape everything that happens before you even take the first step towards your goals. Your self-image is there before you make a plan. If you identify yourself as a risk-averse person and wear this caution with pride, guess how you will go into every new situation? … Cautiously.

Herein the conflict lies – how do you take a leap of faith into the unknown with the possibility of an amazing life, if you think of yourself as highly risk averse? Well, you can't – that particular self-image is limiting and self-fulfilling.

In order to achieve all the goals you set out in Chapter 3, you need to ferociously believe that you are capable of doing so. You need to have the self-esteem, confidence and trust in yourself. You need to be proud of who you are. When your self-image is conducive to success, then you can go for your goals with such gusto that nothing will stop you. When you start peeling away the layers of conditioning and tap into your Soul for guidance, your unique talents and gifts will surface and lead you to fulfil your passion and purpose in life. I truly believe that we all have unique talents and that, if we let ourselves, we can use them to create our most abundant life.

The hardest part in changing our self-image is that it is buried in our subconscious, which, after all, runs 80 per cent of what we do, and it takes some digging deep. You may be asking: 'But how do I change this?' You may be looking at your list of goals and all you can think of is how you have 'failed' in the past. Well, one insanely powerful way of loosening the psychological hold that your past has over you is by judging all your future-based goals in terms of your new identity (and not your old one), the identity that you have chosen for yourself. You will become the person who can achieve those goals once you let go of the person who has 'failed' in the past.

How I chose to change

I had made the choice to change how I saw myself around two weeks prior to receiving the news that marked the beginning of the radical change in my life. I was on a plane to Hawaii full of excitement about the week ahead on a paradise island that had been patiently sitting on my bucket list for a decade. I was finally going there. I had brought some light reading, a book by the incredibly wise Wayne Dyer called *The Power of Intention*. I'll never forget the words he wrote that jumped off the page letter by letter and tattooed themselves firmly on the organ between my ears: 'All situations are emotionally neutral. We can decide how we feel about any given situation.'

Those were the words that would save me from a downward spiral over the coming weeks.

As I landed on the beautiful island of Oahu, I had no idea that the next few weeks would chokeslam the fuck out of me and cause me to be reborn as the woman I am today.

As I walked down to breakfast with my kids and husband in tow, ready to casually order my fresh orange and poached eggs, my phone rang. It was my sister. I felt something inside me tell me that something bad was about to happen and I was right.

I held back the tears while shielding my face behind my break-fast menu so my daughters wouldn't see me break down. My sister delivered the devastating news that my youngest brother, who was eight at the time, had been diagnosed with leukaemia. 'He's riddled with infection and cancer' were her words.

I felt sick. You never think it will happen to your family.

I looked at my two beautiful girls, who were just a few years younger than my brother, and the stab of pain in my heart almost took my breath away. I imagined the news being deliv-ered about my own children. I couldn't hold the tears back knowing that, at that moment, my dad must have felt that his world was falling down around him.

After several phone calls back and forth to the UK, I made the decision to carry on with our plans to visit a waterfall and go for a hike. That day I swam in a beautiful waterfall and I chose to do something that most people wouldn't understand. I kept repeating, 'I am grateful.' I had to believe that there was a greater lesson, something wonderful *had* to be at the end of this holy mess.

There was something deeply comforting about appreciating the majesty of nature, even in a moment of total distress. I had to believe that this piece of news was a gift in ugly wrapping and that the gift would make itself known after time. I chose to be the person who saw the good in even the darkest of times. I chose to see the situation as emotionally neutral and attach a positive feeling to it.

Did it stop the hurting? No. Did it make my brother better within a week or remove the need for an agonizing course of chemotherapy? No. Did it give me hope? Absafuckinglutely.

You see, you can choose to be a Debbie Downer, a victim, a gossip queen or the person who moans because that is what they are used to doing. But when you choose to tap into love and gratitude, you open the doors for your pure potential and the ability to manifest that what you want. I badly wanted my brother to get better, and months later, against the odds, he was in full remission. That six months could have been full of negativity, anger and fear. They could have been full of love. I chose love.

What you need to understand is that the Soul's default mode is love (there's more on your Soul in the next chapter). The more we are kind and joyful and make the care of, and service to, others our priority, we quieten the Ego. Love, kindness and joy are like kryptonite to the Ego. It cannot survive them. Those positive emotions set the stage for your Soul to communicate with you and help you tap into its excellent guidance. When you moan, groan, bitch and complain, Ego knows that this is its jam and, *oomph*, it will appear on cue and start running the show with gusto again.

It's also imperative that you learn to see the possibilities in spite of how dark or dreary life seems.

You have a choice: to be the person who sees everything as an opportunity or the person who sees everything as an opportunity to beat yourself up. If you let yourself be beaten up, it doesn't matter how well you do in life. So ...

- You have achieved great sales? You'll always find a way to berate yourself for not getting more.
- You're in a wonderful relationship? You'll always find a way of focusing on the 10 per cent that's missing.
- You're feeling in the best shape after a year of personal training? You'll always look for the flabby bits.

It's important to shift your thinking from that which is led by fear or doubt or negativity to that which is empowering and positive. There will always be duality in life that is ever present and inevitable. Where there is light, there is dark; where there is wet, there is dry; where there is good, there is bad; where there is a bottle of champagne, there is an empty glass. Of course, in every situation above, as in life, you can always choose to accept the reality, the duality, and move on to see the possibility.

It really is time for that spiritual facelift

Now, it's time for you to choose who you want to be. Let's start the process of removing your emotional scars, amending your attitude and repairing your thought processes. It's time to remove your beliefs of lack, loss, failure resentment and forgive yourself. I give you full permission to take on a new identity, of someone who 'thinks that you can'.

We were created for a reason and, whatever beliefs you hold around creation, it does not make sense that we were created to fail. Nothing is intentionally created with the goal of failing. Each and every one of us is *designed* for success and, when we embody that belief in our identity, our thoughts then create actions that lead us to success.

We were not designed to fail. We were not put on this planet to have anything less than that which we wish for. Our default 'factory setting' at birth was programmed to succeed. We humans were put on this planet to thrive, and as long as you know the end results you want and how to become the person you need to be to go for them, then the world is your big, glistening oyster. But you need to reset your programming.

Your new identity will shape everything you do. There are many ways in which to start creating this identity. And none of them depends on actually achieving anything, so don't worry about your recent track record:

- Choose to be awesome.
- Choose to have confidence.
- Choose to be successful.
- Choose to be smart.
- Choose to be disciplined.
- Choose to be sexy.
- Choose to be fearless.
- Choose to be inspiring.
- Choose to be classy.
- Choose to be sassy.
- Choose to be a little badassy.

It doesn't really matter who you choose to be – I just want you to fucking do it, my darling.

One of the most powerful ways to reprogram our self-image is through visualization. We are the only species on the planet that has been given the gift of imagination. Imagination allows us to create and dream. This is an important part of the manifestation puzzle because the only difference between the successful people out there and the unsuccessful ones is the choice they make about what they think about. Because, as I have explained, our thoughts become things.

Let me give you an example of the power of imagination. For one moment, I just want you to take a deep breath in. Now I want you to imagine that you go to your fruit bowl and you see a nice big juicy yellow lemon. I want you to pick it up, go get a knife and cut it in half. I want you to imagine licking and sucking on it. What happens? Can you feel your lips pursing? Can you taste the sourness of the imaginary lemon? Yes? Your mind, you see, doesn't know the difference between reality and imagination.

Neuroplasticity refers to the brain's ability to form new neural pathways (interconnections between parts of our nervous system). As with building muscle, the more we 'work out' certain neural pathways, the stronger they become. Strong pathways become our favoured psychological 'highways', and so by using our imagination through visualizations that are also attached to strong emotion, we can create new ways of thinking and being.

When we visualize on a regular basis, we actually create new 'memories' that replace the 'old', stored memories of our past identity that weren't serving us. Even though these new 'memories' aren't reality in the physical world, your brain does not know the difference and will start to work to help you to move towards your desired outcome. The more precise you are, the stronger your vision will be, and the more you empower your brain to come up with ways to turn that vision into reality.

'What you imagine, you create,' said the Buddha.

TOP TAKEAWAYS

- Your beliefs about who you are shape your identity. They govern every action you take in your life.
- You are born with the capacity and power to do something awesome until conditioning moulds you into something else.
- You need to recognize where along the way you have been shaped into someone you perhaps don't want to be. You must be restored to 'factory settings'.
- Peeling back the layers and removing the mask is crucial for tuning into the right frequency for manifesting.
- Your past identity will not be the identity that takes you to the new phase of your rock star life. It's time to create a self-image that is conducive to success.

JFDI!

Practise the art of visualization

In Chapter 5 you considered what you believed you had failed at. You investigated who had set the yardsticks of that failure for you.

Now I want you to dig a little deeper and write down *why* you wouldn't be able to get to your goals. What are your fears? What personality traits would stop you? What are the limiting beliefs that you hold at your core? I want you to write down everything that comes into your mind, even if it seems inferior or silly.

Next I want you to go through your list and repeat the words 'I forgive myself, I love myself', as you cross out each one of these fears, traits and beliefs. You need to say this out loud so as to start reprogramming your subconscious.

Now you can start creating 'new' memories and a strong mental picture of who you choose to be moving forward. Really think about the goals you set out for yourself.

Who do you need to be to achieve those goals?

I knew I needed to be disciplined. I knew I needed to be courageous.

Get super-duper clear on the person who has achieved the goals you set out:

- How do they show up in the world?
- What are their personality traits?
- What are they doing day to day?
- How is their physical body?
- What do people say about them?

Once you have crafted your 'mind movie' of your new chosen identity, you need to spend 15 minutes a day visualizing this.

Visualize yourself celebrating the manifestation of your intentions as already accomplished. If it's your relationsh want to fix, picture yourself vividly enjoying the relationship you dream of. If it's weight loss you desire, imagine yourself working out at the gym and enjoying it. If it's a successful business, mentally picture yourself doing deals, celebrating milestones and banking large sums of money. Imagine yourself showing up as the best version of yourself.

Breaking through negative chatter while visualizing takes practice. At first, when you try to do it, it will seem difficult and demanding. But if you start small and try it repeatedly every day, you will gradually become stronger. And, before long, it will become effortless. If it helps, listen to some music that inspires you. Remember, when we attach each positive emotion to a visualization, it creates those new neural pathways.

Have patience and the results will astound you. Oh, and if you think this sounds like hassle to take 15 minutes out of your day to do this, then shame on you. Excuses are dream thieves – so just fucking do it!

7

Choose Yourself

We currently have an epidemic of extreme self-love deficiency which has resulted in millions of people treating themselves pretty badly.

OK, now you have uncovered your stories and chosen to embrace a new self-image, it is time to strengthen that self-image and cement it in, just like a star on the Hollywood Walk of Fame.

So, let me ask you something: do you believe in yourself? Let me go further: do you love yourself? This isn't a trick question where you answer yes, and I then point and laugh and call you an egotistical big head. I am being deadly serious.

Why do I ask this? Well, self-love was a term I only heard in my late twenties. Self-hate was something I was pretty good at practising and I've noticed the same among the general population. 'I am so fat', I would ruthlessly tell myself on repeat. I would secretly resent the size-6 girls around me, wishing they would binge-eat McDonald's Big Macs and put on weight to make me look like the slim one! For me to control what I was eating seemed much harder than the self-loathing and cycles of crazy-ass dieting that led me down a long dark road to absolutely nowhere. Your body is meant to be a temple, but mine was more like a kebab shop.

I spent most of my mid-teens and early twenties yo-yo dieting, dabbling in suspicious diet pills that I purchased online, and, shamefully, even contemplating how to make cotton wool palatable as I had read that models ate it to make them full, with zero calories. Serious shit goes down when you hate the body you live in. We don't punish, berate, condemn or consider stuffing ourselves like one of those toys at Build-A-Bear if we love ourselves. We don't punish our bodies with excessive alcohol, narcotics and highly processed fast food on a regular basis if we respect the only body we are given.

We currently have an epidemic of extreme self-love deficiency which has resulted in millions of people treating themselves pretty badly. Self-love isn't some airy-fairy, namby-pamby, sunshine crap meant only for girls or boys who have lost their balls – it's important. A lack of self-love and self-belief is linked to a plethora of psychological problems from underachievement at school and work to anxiety and depression, alcohol and substance abuse.

A personal experience

I have seen at first-hand how a lack of self-love can tear people's lives apart, because it results in suffering. It was winter 2010 and I was staying at my family home and enduring yet another night of emotional bullying by a man who supposedly loved us. My mum had gone out and left me at home with my stepdad and I overheard him on the phone saying how awful we all were. He was in an intoxicated state. I felt my blood boiling. I ran downstairs and I saw the bottle of vodka on the side and grabbed it. I frantically took the lid off and started pouring it down the sink. I was shaking from a mixture of anger and adrenaline at the fear of being caught, but this bottle was the antagonist in all of our lives.

In a sudden flash, my stepdad came running over, his face so red I thought it was going to explode. 'What are you doing?' he bellowed. I started screaming at him: 'It is KILLING YOU.' I was fighting back the tears and still shaking from the adrenaline coursing through my blood.

I looked at him towering over me ready to strike. 'Hit me, then,' I shouted. 'Go on and then I can call the police and you can finally be out of here.'

He stopped in his tracks, threw some more verbal abuse at me and walked away. I ran upstairs and wept. How had this amazing man whom we loved so dearly turned into this monster? The man who married our mother and who we so proudly called our stepdad. A man who used to treat us like family.

My stepdad was an alcoholic. I say 'was' because only a few days ago, as I write this, he sadly passed away with a terminal liver disease. I hear on a daily basis that alcoholism is a disease and almost out of the addict's control. Yep, a disease of the mind. A disease where suffering turns into a way of life and where the only way out for someone is to anaesthetize the pain with a litre of vodka a day.

My stepdad had lost his self-belief. He had no self-love and believed that the world was out to get him. He had lost control in his suffering. Please understand that he was not a horrible man. He had been possessed by the pain of his own self-loathing. Suffering is always linked to how someone *thinks* about a situation and my stepdad had learned to become helpless, refusing to believe he was good enough, and medicated this feeling with alcohol. One of my motivations when I became a coach was to help people understand that the meaning we give to a situation can help us move past it. That even in our darkest moments, we have a choice to change how we think. That, however difficult, there is always an opportunity to see it through different eyes.

The truth about self-love

There is real irony here because growing up we are taught that 'loving yourself' is a negative thing and we associate it with being big-headed, narcissistic or egotistical. But when we love ourselves fully, we don't treat our body and mind like an enemy. If it were possible to record the things I would tell myself in my head when I was depressed, most people would be appalled, yet so many of us have a playlist of punishing phrases on repeat inside our skulls, berating the one person we are stuck with for life. Yep, we are stuck with ourselves till death do us part so we should be way nicer to ourselves.

Self-love goes way deeper than running yourself a hot bath or treating yourself to a handbag. Self-love is the ability to be really honest with yourself about what you aren't happy about so you can actually sort it out. Self-love is accepting and owning all parts of your story – however dark those chapters may be. Self-love is accepting your whole journey and the person it's made you instead of condemning yourself for not getting it right. Self-love is having the discipline to go for what you really want – whether that's loving yourself more in order to leave the partner who is making you miserable, finally quitting the sugar that is giving you diabetes, or actually going for your dreams so you can be the happiest version of you.

A lack of self-love could be less in your face than alcoholism and lurk more deeply in your subconscious. You might be holding a belief at your core that you are not worthy of the money, the love or the body you desire, which then manifests as you subconsciously take actions that sabotage your success.

The level of love that you have for yourself will determine the actions that you decide to take. If you don't believe you are worthy of financial abundance, you are less likely to take the risks necessary to build your finances or to take the leap of faith to start that business or go for that promotion. If you don't see that you are deserving of perfectly toned abs or a J-Lo booty, you are less likely to put the time into working out, since 'it's all a waste of time and money and won't help anyway'. If you do not believe you are worthy of that 'happily ever after', you are more likely to either withhold your love or turn into a total psychopath who ends up subconsciously creating arguments in an attempt to break up the relationship at every twist and turn.

I'm guilty as charged on all of the above. How about you?

Self-love is not something that you are born with or born without. It does not depend on how successful you are, and it is not a personality trait. Loving yourself is a way of life, a daily ritual – a practice. The truth is, lots of people look at me now and see a happy, bubbly, successful, confident woman because they don't see the war wounds. I have spiritually lasered away the scars of my past and they are not detectable to the naked eye. They are there, though. But instead of letting the pain define me, I have let it teach me. Instead of holding on to the past which resulted in me punishing myself, I have learned to forgive myself so I can truly move forward. I made a decision to love myself, not just like myself, because loving myself is so much more powerful. You too can choose to shamelessly believe in and love yourself.

So how do you make that all-important shift from the clutches of condemnation into the happier, more loving relationship with the one person you spend all your time with? Well, Step 1 is forgiving yourself for the past – letting go of anything that has to led you to believe today that you are unworthy. Step 2 is embracing life in spite of the fear (which shows up in various forms) because you love yourself enough to go and find that biggest version of yourself. And Step 3 is respecting your journey enough to be grateful for all the highs, the lows and the three loop-the-loops that got you here.

'As you love yourself, life loves you back,' writes Kamal Ravikant in *Love Yourself Like Your Life Depends on It*. 'I don't think it has a choice either. I can't explain how it works, but I know it to be true.'

Let's talk about the F-word

As you may have gathered, I like words beginning with f, but it's not just the 'rude' ones. I happen to have two other F-words that I think are pertinent in this magical journey of self-discovery. The first is faith (we have covered that already, in Chapter 2) and the second is forgiveness.

Forgiving yourself and also forgiving others in spite of what they have done is one of the hardest actions on the path towards self-love that we can take. You see, when you embrace this loving yourself malarkey, it shows that you are willing to put your own energy first. Holding on to your resentment towards others because they weren't good enough in your eyes affects your energy mojo terribly, which in turn affects your ability to create a much more abundant life.

SARAH'S STORY

Take Sarah. When Sarah was five years old, her mother left her to be brought up by her much older and retired father. From the ages of five to 13, she only saw her mother once a year. She went to a school in a nice area where everyone seemed to have a lot of money and, in Sarah's words, belonged to 'perfect' families with 'normal' lives.

Sarah felt uncherished and unloved compared to her friends, and she started to form a belief that she wasn't good enough to be loved, which was why, she thought, her mother had left. She carried this horrible thought lodged in her subconscious until she was 35.

When we started working together she told me she was scared of having a successful business. As I delved deeper, it became clear that she didn't really believe she deserved the success because she didn't believe she was good enough. Let's face it, if you didn't feel loved by those who brought you into the world, why would you learn to love yourself or believe in yourself?

Her fear of success was just a way of keeping herself small. She needed to forgive her parents, let go of any resentment and make peace with the fact that these beliefs she had formed were totally false. There was a little girl inside Sarah who needed some loving and healing, and that meant taking the time to acknowledge that her self-worth as an adult had nothing to do with how she was treated as a child.

I wonder whether you can relate to Sarah's story. I know I can. When I was 11 years old, my life changed when two girls of the same age and very close to me confided in me that they had been sexually abused. They swore me to secrecy, and as a loyal 11-year-old I kept schtum. Even though I was only

11, I remember fully understanding the gravity of what sexual abuse was. I inherently knew that something very, very wrong had happened and cried hysterically when I found out. But I promised to keep it a secret and consequently felt a level of responsibility that no 11-year-old child should have to bear.

As I grew older, the secret became heavier. It caused me to have terrifying nightmares, but I could never tell people why. I felt a palpable level of guilt that I had let these girls down. Of course, I hadn't. I was 11 years old, but I created a deep-rooted belief which then manifested in me developing the first signs of depression when I was about 12. I lived with this secret for almost a decade before reaching out to tell someone. Shortly after, the perpetrator died and so got away with it. The anger and the guilt festered inside me for years to come and subconsciously I didn't believe that I was deserving of success.

When I was 12 my parents divorced. Unlike for most children, this was a welcome change. I had lived in a war zone for most of my childhood and had been caught in between two parents who had no clue how to make each other happy. During this time, I was also getting bullied at school by a girl who was determined to make my life a misery. I went to a girls' school and ... well, girls can be pretty nasty. This girl would go out of her way to exclude me and, as someone who suffered from a chronic need to be loved and accepted, this hurt like hell. I'll never forget the time that one of the girls had a party and proceeded to invite everyone in my year, bar me. It seems so trivial now but at the time it felt like a physical punch in the face. I still to this day don't know what she found so offensive about me. I had never really fitted in with any of the cliques, and I remember always feeling deeply uncomfortable as I was always trying hard to conform.

Aged 16, I fell in love for the second time. He was five years older and drove a car, which made him super-cool, and initially he made me feel like a million dollars. The kudos of dating an older guy gave me serious street cred at school and elevated my status from total loser to at least slightly cool. And he made me laugh and I loved him.

But things started to unravel quickly. I started to drink a lot at the weekends, especially as I could get into pubs and clubs because I was with my older boyfriend. He was very controlling, emotionally manipulative and insanely jealous, and he used my heart as a punchbag. There was an incident when we were in the pub and I was talking to one of his friends. He walked up to me and started calling me names and then proceeded to pour a whole pint of beer over me: 'No one will like you now,' he sneered. I remember the devastating humiliation and the belief that he was right. And yes, like most girls who don't value themselves, I stuck around for more because I loved him.

The lowest point was waiting in the hospital as he had his stomach pumped after he tried to commit suicide by overdosing. Thank God he survived, but soon after he told me that it was my fault that he had wanted to kill himself. With his threats of suicide and the petty humiliations he inflicted on to me, he co-opted me into his own internal emotional warfare. That's when I started to develop anxiety and a lot of bad thoughts. It felt like I had an invisible emotional cord that bound me to him, and the cord was just getting tighter and tighter and I didn't know how to untie myself. This boy I loved so deeply I also hated deeply.

I kept wondering why everything, even at the age of 16, felt so hard. If life was this hard, I wasn't sure that I wanted to participate any more. By the time I was 16, I was on Prozac®. I distinctly remember being in my GP's surgery and explaining to her that I just didn't feel like I could go on. There were days when I felt fine and happy (usually if I was out getting drunk) but most days I just felt low. I actually stopped taking the antidepressants after a month and I finally ended that toxic relationship months later after he turned physically abusive one evening.

I desperately wanted someone to notice me and love me, to help me feel better. I had developed a deep-seated anxiety that I later realized stemmed from a fear of people hurting me. I was so frightened that I wasn't good enough, and I couldn't bear the feeling of heartbreak that comes with rejection. The anxiety was sometimes so unbearable that I could barely breathe, and my heart would pound so hard I was convinced that it would break through my chest and split me in half.

The anxiety was strongest when I was in relationships, yet ironically I was so desperate for love that I went from one relationship to another. It was a vicious cycle in which I truly believed that my happiness lay in the hands of another person. I was always waiting for Prince Charming to come and make me feel truly happy, and yet every time I entered a new relationship the anxiety would return. Although there were some wonderful times, I always found myself dealing with an undercurrent of fear that this person would hurt me or leave me. Naturally enough, this fear made me act like a total looney, and consequently each and every one of those relationships ended, leaving me depleted and drained.

At 20 years old, when I was dumped yet again, I discovered the greatest antidote to pain – cocaine. It felt great to anaesthetize the suffering. I was someone else every time I snorted a line of that white powder; I was strong, powerful, carefree and fun. I was the life and soul and my confidence was on another level. I was popular and funny and outrageous. I could look my ex in the eye and send him a metaphorical 'Fuck you', even though inside I desperately wanted him back.

Soon after, I also started using ecstasy. I was having fun and going out as much as I could. It gave me the excuse to get high as a kite. But where there is an up there is always an almighty down. The comedowns were horrific. My anxiety worsened, my low days became lower and I started suffering from insomnia and leg spasms. As anybody who has experienced insomnia knows, it's nothing short of torture to be awake all night with only your own thoughts.

I was a party girl, but it was only in hindsight that I realized that the fun was there as a distraction from myself. And, quite honestly, I didn't like myself at all. I hated my body, I hated the fact I was single, and I hated the fact I had anxiety because it was ruining all my relationships. So, you see, I understand how easy it is to fall out of love with yourself. I felt like my life was a mess.

I know that I'm not alone in my experience. Most of us have such a fraught relationship with ourselves that we look for love and happiness from outside of ourselves. We base our joy on the validation and acceptance given by others. Depending on others to make you happy, as I did, is hugely disempowering and results in you becoming needy, possessive and jealous.

I finally learned that, until I loved myself, I would never truly feel the happiness of being loved by another. So many people think that we need to be in love with another person to shine, whereas, in fact, it's when we learn to love ourselves *first* that we truly blossom.

When I started a brand-new relationship with me, that was when my marriage changed for the best and I engaged in a deeper, more respectful relationship based on mutual appreciation instead of reliance.

Forgiving yourself

All of the experiences I went through put a mental stamp on my brain, and all your experiences will have done the same. So, forgiving yourself is really crucial. Your pain and mistakes, when properly examined, can become your spiritual director, and it's actually those times of great distress that will provide you with an opportunity to find your inner gold and the lessons that will help you become the best version of yourself.

I want you to write down a list of mistakes you have made in your life. Things you regret. Things that you wish you had done differently.

Now I want you to write what you learned from each of them.

Now go through each one, cross it out and repeat: 'I forgive myself, I love myself.'

Forgiving others

The people who cause us pain or anger – *they* are our most important teachers. They are the ones who indicate the limits to our capacity for forgiveness. Blaming others or, even worse, blaming yourself for things in the past will not help you move forward into the future, and so it is incredibly important for you to acknowledge that, as well as forgiving yourself, you also have to forgive those you feel have wronged you.

Forgiveness does not make what they did right. It doesn't mean you negate the fact that what they have done is wrong. To forgive someone is you powerfully saying, 'I no longer choose to hold on to the bad energy that this resentment or blame is giving me.' It's about you choosing to love yourself more than your anger and pain.

I want you to write down a list of people who have hurt you and towards whom you still hold some negative energy.

Now I want you to write a letter a forgiveness to each of them. You don't need to give it to them if you don't want – this is more about you taking it out of your brain and putting it down on to paper. This conscious acknowledgement of forgiveness will be powerful.

Remember, true happiness comes when you can be thankful for an experience, whether it's positive or negative, and forgiveness is an important part of this thankfulness. In order for you to move forward, you must let go of all the pain in the past.

Don't fake it till you make it

Choosing to love yourself takes courage as it requires you to accept your truth, accept your story and understand that you have the power to change it. Keeping up the pretty picture that your life is perfect when internally you feel the opposite will leave you feeling emotionally and mentally depleted.

While reading this book you may have gathered by now that one of my dreams was to be on stage. So, when I got offered the opportunity to be an extra in a film, I jumped at the chance. No, I wouldn't get a starring role, but I would finally get to experience what it was like to be in a film. I was flown out to Spain to take part in a scene on a boat in *The Inbetweeners*. If you were to watch the film now and flick through to the boat party scene, you would see sunshine, dancing, happy faces and a glorious scene of teenage debauchery on holiday.

The reality on set was a very different story. First, it was freezing, as there was a cold wind blowing. The boat was filled with fake-tanned extras fighting over big brown blankets to keep themselves warm and popping seasickness tablets in an attempt not to throw up on one other. Sometimes filming five minutes of the final film would take hours of shooting. The whole experience, in short, was a far cry from the glamorous lifestyle I had pictured as a child.

It was that week that I finally dropped the dream of being an actress. Truth be told, a lot of people keep up this pretence that their life is the perfectly edited blockbuster when behind the scenes they are cold, sick and huddling glumly under a blanket: the woman who refuses to share with her friends that her husband is cheating for fear of being judged; the man who puts on the front of a happy marriage to cover up the fact that he's gay; the lawyer who goes home and drinks every night because his successful career is burning him out.

Trying to keep your shit together and be perfect is exhausting. Keeping up appearances for fear that someone may see the *real* you is a sure-fire route to end at misery hotel. Self-love means having the honesty and courage to look your life in the eyes without blinking and ask yourself: 'Is this what I truly want? Am I being the person I truly want to be?'

Say no

Loving yourself also means choosing yourself and managing your energy so that you can be as high-vibe as possible and totally in your manifesting lane. Imagine yourself as a generator of energy. You need to be full of positive vibes and every time you choose to do something that doesn't energize you, it's like you are throwing a cord out of your generator which causes an energy leak. You are allowed to be selfish and put yourself first. When you acknowledge that your energy is crucial to your success, you will fiercely prevent any energy leaks happening.

ELLA'S STORY

I would like you to meet Ella. Ella was a chronic pleaser and found it hard to let anybody down. This meant that she was forever saying yes to everyone and everything, which meant she never had time for herself. Not only was this physically draining but also mentally and energetically because every time she had to say yes to something that didn't light her up she felt resentful. When your heart is not in something and you say yes, it's because your Ego is telling you that you are a bad person, so instead of behaving in alignment with your desire, you are acting and faking it.

Stop asking for opinions

One way to trust and love yourself is to drop your need for validation from others. We all do it. That moment in the changing room where you look at yourself in the mirror and secretly think you look epic and yet you still turn to your friend and ask for their opinion. How many times have you asked someone if they prefer your hair one way, or whether they like your outfit, or their opinion on the big life decisions you need to make?

When you honour yourself, you don't wait for someone else to tell you if you look good or are making a good choice. You love yourself enough to make that decision for yourself and embrace it boldly. Yes, there will be occasions when you do truly require a second opinion but make those occurrences a rarity. Get good at validating yourself.

Make every day your birthday!

I explained earlier that self-love is a practice and part of that is celebrating yourself. In this fast-paced world of go-go-go, we don't take a moment to really reflect on how far we have already come. When was the last time you actually just stopped and took the time to celebrate and reward yourself? If you struggle with this idea, you aren't alone.

I used to believe that celebrating yourself only happened on your birthday and even then it was about other people celebrating me. I never just sat down and said, 'Hey, Noor, you've done good.' If you are constantly doing and not being, you will miss out on all the beautiful moments in life. Sometimes, we just take life too seriously and become so attached to the final outcome that we forget to enjoy the journey.

JASMIN'S STORY

Jasmin is an entrepreneur and a mother, and her days get busy. Every morning she would write down a huge to-do list and at the end of the day her mind would become fixated on the things that she hadn't ticked off, instead of the things that she had. Instead of acknowledging and celebrating herself for getting the stuff done, she had fallen into the trap of beating herself up for what she hadn't.

This is a big middle finger up to the Universe and a sure-fire way of tuning in to ShitFM. Don't wait until you've reached your goals to give yourself a round of applause. When you take time every day to acknowledge the little actions that you are taking towards the achievement of your goals, you strengthen those actions. The Universe *loves* a party and every time you congratulate yourself for getting through a day and moving closer towards your goals, you are tuning in to the right frequency.

When you celebrate your successes, it will motivate you to achieve more, which in turn will skyrocket your confidence. When you do so, you are telling the Universe that you are unstoppable, and this, in turn, attracts more positive energy into your life. Are you ready to own your amazingness?

You deserve to have your accomplishments recognized even if they are small. If you don't celebrate yourself, then who will?

TOP TAKEAWAYS

- Self love is more than just running a bath. It's a deep appreciation for yourself and all of your story.
- Until you love yourself, you will never fully allow your deepest desires to appear.
- Forgiveness of yourself and others is crucial.
- It's OK to say no and be selfish.
- Celebrate yourself, every goddamn day.

JFDI!

Dance like nobody is watching!

Spend one minute every day celebrating your life – make every day your birthday. It will put you into a high vibrational state. Go to your list of goals and write down one thing you will do for yourself every time you achieve each one – whether that's to buy a gift, have a glass of champagne or book a trip away, just decide how you will celebrate.

Life is not a race. When you learn to find the fun in the journey, the destination feels all the more worthwhile.

8

Your Word is Your Wand

Your internal and external dialogue is casting spells over your life: sometimes it can be good magic, but it can also be very, very black magic indeed.

I used to play this game when I was younger. It was called 'I have never …'. It usually involved a few friends and a bottle of some cheap booze I'd bought on a trip abroad, for less than 5 euros, and which tasted of methanol. The rules of the game are simple. Each player is armed with a drink and has a chance to make a statement that starts with 'I have never' followed by something inappropriate that they have done. Then, if anyone else has also done it, they have to take a gulp of drink. The result is a bunch of drunk, giggly girls who have uncovered their deepest secrets.

Well, I've realized there is a new game we play as adults. It is the 'I could never …' game but in this version we reveal our deepest limiting beliefs. The 'I could never …' game keeps us in a place of staying small and away from living our true potential. For example:

- 'I could never give up sugar' keeps you unhealthy.
- 'I could never leave my job' keeps you unhappy.
- 'I could never leave my partner' keeps you in a toxic relationship.
- 'I could never start that business' keeps you away from your dreams.

You get the gist.

When I became aware that I was playing the 'I could never …' game in my life, I decided it was time to change. Where in your life are you playing this game? As we explored earlier in the book, the beliefs you have formed are creating stories that are limiting you. Changing engrained thought patterns after a decade of conditioning is no easy feat, but using the power of your *words* to help you along the way is crucial and that is what this chapter is all about.

Words, I want you to understand, are potent. Your internal and external dialogue is casting spells over your life: sometimes it can be good magic, but it can also be very, very black magic indeed.

After realizing that I was playing the 'I could never …' game, I became fascinated with understanding how the power of our words and being optimistic versus pessimistic affects our life. Studies have shown that when we say something enough times (internally or externally), we begin to believe it. What comes out of your mouth shapes how you feel … which defines your actions … which has an effect on your outcomes.

The art of hope

I had spent years convincing myself that my life was cursed and, quite honestly, I got so good at being dramatic and shamelessly pulling out the victim card that I wasn't sure how I could change. Richard Bach said, 'Argue for your limitations, and sure enough, they're yours.'

So, when I got into my late twenties and first started dipping my toe into the personal development world and was told that you could prime yourself to cultivate the bright side of life, I was sceptical. Surely, if you could choose to be positive, then everyone would do that?

Well, no.

Perhaps, like me, you have tended to focus on the darker aspects of life, thinking primarily of the worst thing that could happen when you are about to pursue a new business venture or embark on a new relationship. I used to tell myself that New Year's Eve was a cursed night of the year and that things would always go wrong: I have had the heartbreak of being dumped on that night three times to prove that what you believe will happen will happen. I had primed myself to be on the lookout for things going wrong, so the Universe always delivered. Remember, your thoughts become things, and I was manifesting like a mofo but for all the wrong reasons and in all the wrong ways.

Maybe, like me, you have assumed that you'll never get the body you are working towards very early in a new diet or exercise regime. Maybe the idea that things will not work out has stopped you from even trying a new relationship. And perhaps past failures have proved that you were right in thinking such things could never work, which is why you are a willing player in the 'I could never …' game. As I've said before, our minds are designed not to keep us happy but to keep us safe. This means that you are naturally more likely to look for the risks that may hold you back rather than the rewards that will pull you forward.

But let's be real here: in the modern world that most of us live in, we aren't that likely to be ravaged by tigers while doing the weekly grocery shop or bludgeoned by bears en route to the yoga class. It seems like a waste of time and energy to always be carrying out risk assessments.

Don't get me wrong, it's useful in certain situations. For example, I wish I'd risk-assessed before grabbing the microphone at my wedding and blurting out expletives at anyone who wouldn't get on the dance floor – it proved an efficient way of alienating my whole new family only an hour after tying the knot. But it's not so useful as your de facto state of thinking. Why? Because negative thinking leads to negative talk and negative talk almost always leads to negative behaviours.

However, the American psychologist Martin Seligman dared to suggest that new behaviours could be learned by anyone if they employed new cognitive strategies; that is, if you make a habit out of new ways of thinking and talking, you can reverse a pessimistic mindset. Seligman shows that how you explain the situations and challenges you face (both current and future) determines whether you are a half-full or half-empty type of person. This means that, if you change the way that you explain the things that happen to you, then your de facto position can shift from pessimistic to optimistic.

Merriam-Webster's Dictionary neatly defines optimism as 'hopefulness and confidence about the future or the success of something'. In contrast, its definition of pessimism is 'a tendency to see the worst aspect of things or believe that the worst will happen'.

Seligman suggests that you need to study the internal chatter happening inside your own head in order to determine your overall attitude towards life. So, if you learn to consistently change your internal dialogue – or, as Seligman calls it, your explanatory style – then you learn to remain consistently optimistic.

I didn't think I was pessimistic until I took a huge microscope to my conversation, internal and external, and although I had a bubbly disposition, the way I spoke quickly indicated that I was far more pessimistic than I would ever have imagined. I had some serious work to do. From a spiritual perspective, when we change our dialogue, we change our vibe – and by this point in this book, people, you should be super-clear on the result of changing your vibe. How you think about an event determines how you react to it. And how you react to it determines the outcome you get.

Powerfully, how you think about a past event actually determines how you react to future events and so shapes the general tone of your life experience. If you have come from a series of failed relationships, you are more than likely going to take those experiences, make sense of them in a negative way and then subconsciously inscribe the view that all your future relationships won't work. This is an irrational and damaging way of thinking because you have the power to totally change all your future relationships and manifest a long-lasting, happy and fulfilling relationship if you choose to believe and think positively.

The three Ps

There are three dimensions to consider when deciding where you are on the attitude scale:

- Permanence
- Pervasiveness
- Personalization

Let's look at each of these in turn.

Permanence

The first is how permanent you consider situations to be. One of my favourites was 'Diets never work'. As you can see, this is pretty pessimistic as I was using the word 'never'. Believing that bad events will persist and thinking about bad things in terms of 'always' and 'never' indicates that you have a pessimistic explanatory style.

An optimist would see the level of permanence in a much less absolute way, as a temporary setback, so might say, 'Diets never work when I eat out'. As you can see, the optimist reacts to the situation with a sense of personal power and isolates the timeframe to when they go out for dinner rather than all of the time. What's really important is that you understand the opposite also applies. Pessimistic people also see good things that happen as temporary. A pessimist may say things like 'It's my lucky day', which would imply most other days are not.

I didn't want to be pessimistic and, because it is the single biggest determinant of depression, I was happy to get rid of it. Pessimists react to setbacks under the assumption that they had no control over the event and take on a characteristic called 'learned helplessness', reacting to all events using the 'I give up' or the 'No matter what I do, it all fails' paradigm.

This learned helplessness becomes the automatic go-to gear, and, if left to run the show, can have devastating effects. Pessimists consider that bad events are inevitable, will last a long time, undermine everything they ever do and are due to an underlying weakness they have and cannot change. If you continually tell yourself there is no solution to a problem (pessimistic attitude), then the likelihood is that you will not fix it. It's crucial to grasp that even the most optimistic people will feel momentarily helpless when something bad happens, but it's the bounce-back-ability rate from the setback that separates a half-full type of person from the 'my cup is always empty' person.

Pervasiveness

The second dimension to consider when assessing how pessimistic you are is whether you think the setback is specific to that particular situation or not. This is referred to as pervasiveness. Some people can put their troubles away tidily into a box and get on with the rest of their lives, but others can't.

ANNIE'S AND MATTHEW'S STORIES

Annie may have issues with her relationship but will put that away when she's at work and will do well at her job. In contrast, Matthew will turn everything into a catastrophe. When there is one metaphorical cut in his life, it bleeds over everything. Matthew gives up on everything even if the failure has happened only in one area of his life. This is why learned helplessness is one of the strongest correlates of depression because it leaves you feeling constantly vulnerable, scared of being attacked and shuts you off from any opportunities for happiness.

Personalization

The last aspect of explanatory style and for determining how pessimistic you are is whether you decide a problem is internal or external. When bad things happen, we can blame ourselves or we can blame external influences. This is called personalization.

KEVIN'S STORY

Kevin constantly blamed himself that he was struggling to make his business a success. He would internalize the problem and blame it on his being stupid instead of figuring out a solution.

This led him to have low self-esteem. Kevin would speak to himself as if he was speaking to his worst enemy.

It's important to note, though, that we don't want to be blaming others for what happens to us either, and that, from a spiritual perspective, we need to take full responsibility for our journey. So, I will add a caveat here: taking responsibility for a situation and blaming yourself are two very different things. Ultimately, you want to change and so it is imperative that you take on the responsibility for making that change but *without taking it personally* like Kevin.

Responsibility is your ability to respond to a challenge from a place of personal power and growth. Accepting failure as part of a learning curve is the secret to not internalizing things from a negative standpoint. Taking responsibility provides you with the opportunity to dig deep and find a solution from within, instead of blaming yourself.

So, as you can see, there's magic and merit in learning how to whip off your pessimistic pants and slip on a sexy pair of positivity pants with all the trimmings and tassels. These pants will save you from the despair of seeing setbacks as permanent and challenges in life as catastrophes. Ultimately, wearing your positivity pants with pride and learning how to be optimistic is a superpower when it comes to creating your dream life.

Let's get one thing clear: I am a big believer in speaking positively and the power of affirmations, but this doesn't give you permission to blithely ignore the dangers of a future venture. You shouldn't spend your life savings on a risky investment and use the rationale that it's best to be optimistic or start a new business in an industry that you have no clue about just because you have created a set of affirmations. The power of learned optimism is in thinking about things that happen to you in a different way, which leads to you talking about them in a different way, which leads to different actions, which result in an alternative outcome. In essence, you are mastering the art of hope.

You got the power …

The words around you

In addition to changing the way you speak, it's imperative that you take note of the words around you as these have a direct effect on how positive or negative your attitude is. One of the scariest things I started to notice was the amount of sheer pessimism and negativity I was surrounded with on a daily basis. Every time I put on the radio, there was news of another terrorist act. Every time I went on Facebook, there was someone else moaning about the dire state of politics. Every time I switched the TV on, there was another reality show that showcased more broken hearts and cheating partners. Everywhere I turned, there was an opportunity to see the world was a shitty place. I noticed the sheer amount of gossip people around me could engage in, the repetitive statements about how work was dull and the never-ending complaints that so many people were unhappy with their lives. It's easy to see why depression is rife.

I got to thinking how different the world would be if the radio stations broadcast news that shared successes and celebrations instead of misery each hour. Humans, it seems, are obsessed with watching the pain of others. Isn't it a little bit sick that we enjoy watching horror movies and dub this entertainment? And this comes from someone who used to love horror movies. On average, by the time a child is 14, they have seen at least five people killed on TV. Every time we watch those programmes, a low level of cortisol (the stress hormone) is released into our bloodstreams, meaning that we are in a constant state of low-level stress. This, in turn, has adverse effects on our health and body, and it also affects our energy and vibration.

One of the first things I did while on my quest to change my life was to stop listening to the news, stop watching any TV that made me sad or angry, and disconnect from anybody on Facebook who took the time to produce statuses which were negative. I also chose to remove myself from social situations where people preferred to gossip or bitch instead of engaging in meaningful conversation.

This conscious decision to be super-careful about what I let into my brain was, for me, a huge taking back of control. Some people judged me for this, saying that shutting myself off from the 'real' world was actually a kind of selfishness. But switching off the constant flow of negativity doesn't mean that I don't care about what's happening. Quite the opposite: if we are in a negative state that is stopping us from reaching our full potential we certainly won't be able to make a difference to the world's problems.

Personally, too, this cleansing of my consciousness and the decision to shut off negativity from my life were liberating, resulting in my happiness rising, my income rocketing and my free time expanding so I could do more fulfilling things. What's more, I didn't want my children to be exposed to the horror of the world until they were a little older. I'd like them to bask in the ecstasy of being children for as long as they can.

TOP TAKEAWAYS

- Your internal and external dialogues are great indicators of how you go about life.
- You need to study the internal chatter that happens inside your own head in order to determine your overall attitude towards life – the American psychologist Martin Seligman calls it your 'explanatory style'.
- There are three dimensions to consider when deciding where you are on the attitude scale: permanence, pervasiveness and personalization.
- Be aware of what you let into your space: the words around you are shaping your own dialogue.
- Being positive doesn't mean being stupid or risk averse. It just means that you seek out every opportunity for growth and see every challenge through the lens of possibility.

JFDI!

Check your chatter

I want you to get an indication of how you speak to yourself. Grab a piece of paper, or use the notes section at the end of this book, as I have a little task for you.

I want you to think of one area of your life which you are not happy with – perhaps it's your income, your physical health or your relationship. Whatever it is, hold the area of your life you are not happy with in your mind's eye. Then I want you to say out loud, 'It is not good enough.'

Now I want you to write down the words 'This means I'm …' and then complete the sentence. What does it mean to you that you aren't earning enough, or your marriage is failing, or you have let yourself become overweight?

For example:

- 'This means I'm a failure.'
- 'This means I'm a loser.'
- 'This means I'm letting my family down.'
- 'This means I'm stupid.'
- 'This means I'm not loveable.'
- 'This means I'm lazy.'
- 'This means I'm ugly.'

Write whatever comes into your mind.

It's imperative that you allow yourself to write down everything that comes into your mind. The reason this task is so powerful is that it will help you start to recognize the negative self-talk and how damaging it is. Allow yourself to really *feel* the words that you write out.

Now look at your list and imagine that a little child is about to get up and perform the main role in a play, but finds themself ambushed by her teacher, who goes on to criticize every aspect of their acting. Why would that little child be happy and excited about performing after hearing they are a loser or a failure? Could they get on and give their best performance? Of course not, which is why negative self-talk is highly damaging and reinforces the negative connection to the bullshit beliefs you hold about yourself.

Now I want you to flip the switch and change all the negative self-talk you tell yourself into positive affirmations. If you keep telling yourself that you aren't clever enough to start a business, then flip that to 'I am an amazing business owner with all the intelligence I need'. Grab your phone and record each affirmation. I want you to repeat these positive affirmations seven times over. Then listen to them every morning and every night.

9

All Karma is Not Created Equal

Karma is recorded and balanced by the Universe and it never forgets. Loving thoughts, emotions, words and deeds are credits. Negative ones are debits.

Karma is a bitch, you've probably heard. It can well be that, but karma is not about punishment and it should not be viewed this way. It is a powerful energy exchange that keeps us learning. Every time we think, speak or act we're putting energy out into the world that then reflects back to us. Karma is both an action and the consequence of that action; it is cause and effect simultaneously because every action generates a force of energy that returns to us in kind. Simply put, it's 'Give and it will be given to you.'

Simply believing in karma and not acting on that belief has no real effect. It is about as useful as believing in healthy eating without changing your bad diet. You should have a clear understanding of karma and apply that understanding to your life to find inner peace and happiness. When I visited Los Angeles for the very first time back in 2015, I was quite honestly shocked to see the level of homelessness. Every street corner had people living on it. What I have always found quite distressing is people's attitude towards homeless people and the resistance to giving them money on the grounds that 'it will only be used for drugs'. I truly believe that nobody chooses to live their life like that, and compassion should be exercised.

One evening, we walked past a man lying on the sidewalk and my daughter, who was three at the time, asked in sadness why that man didn't have a bed. When I explained to her that not everyone has a home, she asked whether she could give her apple to him. I said, of course she could, and my heart was warmed by her kindness. She left it by his head with a smile on her face and I felt grateful that my child had compassion. Later that day, she asked if we could give some more apples to homeless people, and we gladly obliged by helping her with her quest.

It was a funny exercise with a mixed bag of responses. The first man she pointed at had a clear sign up saying, 'Don't give me money give me drugs'. I didn't think an apple would do and, as I didn't have any crack to hand, we walked past to the next man. He happily took the apple and thanked us for our kindness. We continued walking and Layla pointed at a homeless man sitting at a bus stop. I walked over and said, 'Hey, would you like an apple?' He looked at me in disgust and then opened his mouth, flashing his gums: 'I have no teeth. Give me money.' Despite the fact he had clearly left his manners somewhere along with his teeth, I rummaged in my purse and handed him a five-dollar bill and walked off. I silently blessed him and hoped he would spend the money wisely.

I've made it a rule now that whenever I see anyone who needs help, I'll try to help them out. I want my kids to learn compassion, and I always tell them that, when they do something good, it will come back to them.

Here's another example of karma at work. I was sitting on a train travelling back from university. I was very pregnant, very tired and ready for bed. The ticket man came to me and I told him I had been let on at the barriers as the train was leaving and that I needed to buy my ticket on the train. He took my card and kept saying it was being declined. There was over £10,000 in that account so I knew something funky was happening. He was one of those unforgiving ticket officers, so he then told me I'd need to get off at the next stop, find a cash machine and then catch the next train.

'Are you serious?' I exclaimed.

'Yes, if you can't pay, you need to get off.'

I felt my heart sink. I was exhausted and now I'd miss the kids' bedtime. I felt like shouting some expletives at him or pull out the crying card, but, at that moment, the most beautiful thing happened. The woman behind me flung over a five-pound note, the woman next to me pulled out her purse full of change, and the man across from me got out his bankcard. They all said they would chip in to help me out. My heart was overwhelmed with their kindness. I thanked them all profusely and thanked my karma for coming back to me tenfold.

You see, karma can be your best friend if the actions you put out there are those of love. Whether we like it or not, everything that happens in our lives is a result of a choice we made in the past. Do something good, you get good back; do something bad, you get the bad back. It's as simple as that, folks.

Karma is recorded and balanced by the Universe and it never forgets. Loving thoughts, emotions, words and deeds are credits. Negative ones are debits. And karma always keeps receipts. These are called up by the Universe when we least expect it. When we are unaware of karma we call it fate or luck. You may not get your karma that week or year – it may be a whole decade later – but it will always come. Even bad karma can teach us such great lessons, and it's our job to accept the Universal Intelligence for doing exactly what we need at any given time. Bad karma has lessons that we must learn from in order to pay that Universal debt.

Often spiritual awakenings happen after a time of great pain, and that is exactly what happened to me. You may have to lose your job or your money, experience the loss of someone close or a betrayal by someone you love, or face a full-blown addiction in order to push past the Ego's bullshit. My Ego's bullshit was this fear of not being good enough, which resulted in anxiety. I can categorically tell you that the challenges that bad karma may bring you serve only as an *opportunity* for you to turn inward.

It's your choice to choose

At every moment of our lives we are in that field of all possibilities where we have access to endless choices that will result in different outcomes. However, even though we have the power to be in control of our choices, we have turned into robots with conditioned reflexes that are triggered by people and events resulting in predictable behaviour. These unconsciously. Just like Pavlov's dogs, we respond to stimuli but, because our responses are so automatic, we forget that these are choices that we are making. (The Russian physiologist Ivan Pavlov is famous for showing that when you give a dog food every time you ring a bell, the dog will start to salivate when you a ring bell even in the absence of food. Not too dissimilarly, we humans have a predictable and repetitious response to certain stimuli in our environment.)

The best way to understand and maximize the use of the karmic law is to become consciously aware of the choices you make in every moment. If I were to call you a total loser, you would most likely choose to be offended without realizing that that reaction was a choice. If I were to tell you that you are the best thing since vegan crème brûlée, you would most probably take that as a compliment and be thankful. Either way, it's still a choice, even though the response is automatic.

As part of your Soul-digging journey in this book, you need to make a commitment to start *witnessing* your choices. It's this awareness that will give you a sense of empowerment and a sudden feeling of control as you take this unconscious process into the conscious realm.

When you make any choice, ask yourself two things.

First, 'What are the consequences of this choice that I'm making?'

If you take a second to check in with yourself, you will immediately know what these consequences are. There is a very powerful mechanism that the Universe has to help you make spontaneously correct choices. This is often known as intuition, which I think is one of the best superpowers we humans have. (We will cover this in more detail in Chapter 10.)

This superpower has to do with sensations in your body. Your body experiences two kinds of sensations: one is a sensation of comfort; the other is a sensation of discomfort and is often felt in your gut. Yes, that infamous gut feeling that we have all known but which some people are just too sceptical to follow.

For some, the feeling of comfort or discomfort is in the area of the solar plexus, but for most people it's in the area of the heart. Consciously focus your attention on your heart and ask it what to do. Then wait for the response – a physical response in the form of a sensation. It may be a very faint feeling but it's there.

The second question to ask yourself is: 'Will this choice that I'm making now bring happiness to me and to those around me?' If the answer is yes, then go ahead with that choice. However, if that choice will bring distress either to you or to those around you, then don't make that choice. It's as simple as that. There is only one choice out of all the endless choices available at any given moment that will result in happiness for you and those around you. When you make the right choice, it will result in the right response to every situation as it happens. It's the behaviour that nourishes you and everyone else who is influenced by that action.

Activating good karma

So how do you activate good karma? You need to be positive and have self-respect, which means taking responsibility for your own actions and having respect for others'. You should also offer to correct your mistakes, offer forgiveness, share knowledge and be compassionate. Lastly, when it comes to the result of an action, then the intention behind it is more important than the act itself.

Two people may perform the same task with two different intentions. Someone may start a profit-making business with the pure motive of helping customers fulfil a need, whereas another sells a product simply for money and greed. Only the first one will achieve positive results. The more you bring your choices into your conscious awareness, the more you will spontaneously make those choices which are right – both for you and those around you.

You have the choice to create what you want by harnessing the knowledge that everything in the Universe operates through an exchange. Every relationship is one of give and take because giving and receiving are different aspects of the flow of energy in the Universe. Take the word 'currency', which we use to describe money. If we look at its etymology, we find that it derives from a Latin word meaning 'to run' or 'to flow'. Money is a symbol of the life energy we give and the life energy we receive as a result of the service we provide to others. Circulation keeps it alive and vital and, if we stop the circulation of life energy, it will stagnate. So …

- if you want appreciation, learn to give appreciation
- if you want more money, help others to make more money
- if you want love, learn to give love
- if you want to be blessed with abundance, learn to silently bless everyone with abundance.

The more you give, the more you will receive, because the Universe will always reciprocate your giving. In your willingness to give that which you seek, you will keep the abundance of the Universe circulating in your life. And the best part is, even a thought or simple prayer of giving has the power to transform. This shifts your mindset from scarcity to abundance.

In this busy world where we are so concerned about 'me, me, me', taking a moment to give a gift to everyone you come into contact with may sound like a stretch, but it's the best way to experience how the Universe works.

You may be thinking, 'How can I give to others when I don't have enough myself?' Before you start hollering at me, I am *not* suggesting you buy coffees for total strangers in the queue at your local café. Gifts don't have to be material things. A compliment doesn't cost a dime but can make someone's day feel like a million dollars. Cast your mind back to all the amazing things you have got in your life without having ever asked for them. This is the Universe diligently working in the background.

Paying karmic debt

But let's say you have done some things in the past you're not so proud of and are apprehensive about what shit will hit the fan in the future. Well, I'm here to let you know there are a few ways you can square up your invoice with the Universe.

Option number one is to pay through the suffering brought about by your karmic debt and take the lessons the suffering can give. Yep, suck it up, pal. Or option number two (which is probably more attractive) is to pay it forward using your dharma. You have a unique gift with which you can serve the world and it's your duty in the world to deliver it. This is your dharma. Where karma is what you do to get to the end goal (all your choices that get you to that goal), dharma is your purpose – it is the end goal. Does that make sense? The two concepts or forces are inextricably linked. There's more about your purpose in Chapter 10.

Is your inner child making your choices?

Let me use a client's story to show you the profound effect that understanding your choices can have.

HANNAH'S STORY
Hannah had fallen out with someone who accused of her doing something she hadn't. Hannah immediately reacted with anger and defiance and felt upset and hurt. The situation mentally drained her for days and she couldn't understand why this person was affecting her so much as they weren't even close.

When we spoke, I asked why she was making the choice to feel this way. I knew that this feeling was being triggered by something much deeper rooted, and I asked Hannah whether she recalled a time in her childhood where she had been accused of something that she had not done which induced the same feeling. Almost immediately, she recalled in vivid detail an episode when she was six years old and had got told off by the head teacher and punished for a week for something she had not done. Her strong feelings about the current situation were being driven by her inner child and her past story.

Once Hannah became aware of what was playing out, she had a choice of either letting her inner child run the show and acting in a way that she would regret later, or becoming aware and choosing to react to the situation in an adult way. I helped her to choose to tap into her Soul that would deal with shizzle like a trooper or let her Ego go on a rampage. Sometimes it's easy to feel as though you can't control your reactions because they feel so strong, but I am here to tell you that you have a choice and it's this choice that will affect the outcome.

Hannah decided to internally forgive the person who had wronged her and made the decision to pull herself out of the drama and give her inner child the love she deserved. Hannah told me that she felt immediately lighter. A few short days later, the woman who had wronged her apologized and asked whether they could move on.

When we change our energy and become aware of our choices instead of running on autopilot and letting our feelings or inner child take over, we take power. In order to grow in spirit, we must first become conscious of our thoughts. We only have control over ourselves, what we think and what we feel. Nobody can make us feel a certain way unless we allow them to. When we change who we are within, our heart, mind and everything around us will change too.

Be 'more crab'

I have always thought that crabs were pretty suspicious creatures, walking sideways through life as they do. What I didn't know about the crab is that when it outgrows its shell, the crab sheds it and grows a new one.

I heard this wonderful story about a crab named Grasper.

GRASPER'S STORY

One day, when Grasper's shell fell off, all the other crabs told him he would start hearing voices and to ignore them until his new shell appeared. They wanted Grasper to stay put. Grasper was curious and ventured out from behind his rock despite what his family and friends had told him.

As he ventured out, he came across the biggest crab he had ever seen. He asked the big crab how he had got so big. The big crab said the same thing would happen to him if he allowed himself to give up the small life he knew and learned to grow. The giant crab explained that a crab grows only as large as the world he lives in and as big as the heart inside him. If Grasper was going to be the biggest crab, he would need to widen his horizons. Grasper faced a big choice: to return to his 'safe' little home by the rocks or to step into the biggest version of himself.

The lesson of course is that, if we humans want to become the biggest version of ourselves, we need to make a choice to either stay in the familiar or to let go of our older selves, together with our bullshit stories and small-mindedness, to broaden our horizons. Grasper no longer just wanted to survive; he wanted to break free and see what life really had to offer him. He learned that he had the ability to choose rather than work on autopilot and follow all the other crabs.

Life mirrors all that surrounds around us, and what surrounds us mirrors life. This is a universal truth and applies to everything in this existence. We must learn to take responsibility for ourselves and our circumstances. Things are neither good nor bad – these are just the labels we put on them. Everything that happens to us happens in order to help us and we must take responsibility in order to grow. And it doesn't matter what took you to that point, just remember it's a chance to cleanse yourself and reconnect with your deepest purpose.

TOP TAKEAWAYS
. . . .

- Karma is not a bad thing or a punishment and works for both positive and negative choices.
- The best way to understand and maximize the use of the karmic law is to become consciously aware of the choices you make in every moment.
- Your body experiences two kinds of sensations: comfort and discomfort (this one you feel in your gut).
- Activating good karma starts with the good intention behind any choice. The more you give the more you receive.
- Be more crab and know that, in order to grow, you may outgrow those around you.

JFDI!

Activate good karma

In this JFDI! task you are going to intentionally activate good karma. The simplest and easiest way to do this is by giving self-lessly to others, and one of my favourite ways to do this is by 'random acts of kindness'.

For 24 hours, see how many times you can go out of your way to do something extra kind. A random act of kindness can be simply sending someone who is standing in front of you at the checkout in the supermarket a blessing in your head. You could silently wish for them to have a good meal with the food they have bought. It could be buying a homeless person a coffee. It could be calling up a friend and asking them whether they need any help with something. It doesn't matter. but the idea is that, for 24 hours, you become consciously aware of others and the ways in which you can give.

Kindness to others actually results in a positive chemical change in our bodies as well as in other people's. In a world where everyone is so me, me, me, see how many people you can make smile by thinking about them. I'll warn you, this can be quite addictive!

Being kind to others is easy, so just fucking do it! I'd also love you to share what you have done on social media with the hashtag #jfdibekind, and let's become more conscious about how we can make a difference (even in a small way) to the lives of those around us.

10

Google Doesn't Know All the Answers

Praying is speaking to the Universe; intuition is the Universe speaking to you.

You are armed with superpowers of which you probably are not even aware, and which can lead you to your most epic life. I've talked about the ability to use your thoughts to manifest, but another superpower that all too often gets taken for granted and is hugely underused is your *intuition*.

Your intuition is a natural gift and internal GPS which is known by different names – hunch, inspiration, ideas, instinct, sixth sense and gut feeling, among them. The word 'intuition' comes from the Latin *intueri* ('to look into') and in English was originally used for spiritual inspection, so that it means something like 'to go inside to learn the answers'. It operates outside the normal parameters of experience and cannot be seen, heard, smelled, or tasted, but is designed to guide you effortlessly towards the life you keep imagining.

Your intuition is a vehicle for your highest, best-est, badass-est self to communicate with you, and if you listen, it's whispering in a loving voice … 'Just fucking do it!' Intuition taps into the cosmic computer – the field of pure potentiality, pure knowledge and infinite organizing power – and takes everything into account. At times it may not even seem rational, but your intuition has a computational ability that is far more accurate and far more precise than anything within the limits of rational thought. It is the spiritual faculty that does not need to explain, but simply knows exactly what you need to do in order to make your dream life a reality and will happily guide you every step of the way.

Soul-ar power

Your intuition is literally like the Universe phoning you or your Soul speaking to you. Once you are in tune with this, you become powered by Universal Intelligence which is the most powerful energy out there: you basically become 'Soul-ar-powered'!

Your Soul knows what you want, has your best interests at heart and is always bloody right. In those times when you are scared about stepping into your bigger life, it's the part of you that wants to hold your hand and tell you to take a leap of faith into the unknown. It will communicate with you by a hunch that encourages you to go in a certain direction. It can lead you to safety in times of chaos, can encourage you to step into new opportunities during times of uncertainty, and can lead you to a world beyond that which you experience with your other five senses. And while everyone has intuition, the process of learning to trust it is an entirely different story.

Have you ever had a moment when you felt as though something was a little shady for your liking? Perhaps you feel negative around someone without knowing why? And if you've experienced this before, have you shrugged it off, dismissing it as illogical nonsense? Or perhaps the total opposite happened: you had this overriding feeling that you absolutely *had to* do something, and it turned out to be the best decision ever, yet you can't pinpoint *why* you actually did it. Pretty much everyone has experienced those moments when unconscious reasoning makes us do something without telling us why or how.

The problem is, for far too long, the noise of that pesky little Ego has been drowning out the whisperings of your Soul. The Ego is noisy. It's like a two-year-old who never grows up and will relentlessly stamp his feet and beat his fists until you give in. Ego wants you to be consistently concerned with the world outside, and yet the secret to tapping into your total potential and listening to the guidance coming from your Soul is to learn how to turn your gaze inward. You need to ignore Ego's crazy voice.

The thing about us humans is that we tend to listen to all the noise. The world is so insanely noisy that you need a huge pair of totally pimped-up noise-cancelling headphones to do this inner work of connecting with your Soul. There's the noise of your own mind, the noise of the people around you, the noise of your culture, the noise of your conscience, the noise of expectations. Not many of us actually take time out of our busy lives, our filled-up inboxes, our scrolling newsfeeds, to just sit still and quieten the cacophony of interfering noises and let our Soul show us the way.

We need to give it space to do that. It won't keep fighting with the Ego. You need to give it *permission* to take centre stage and allow it to dance inside you. You need to learn to ignore the successes or failures of the outside world and commit to being totally focused and healthily obsessive about your own journey.

Even if the Ego has more power right now, we are totally going to change that in this chapter. When you awaken your Soul, you are tapping into the power of pure potential that lies dormant within you. When you become obsessed by your own personal growth as it relates to you, rather than personal growth in relation to the success of others, you can start manifesting things beyond your wildest dreams.

How to tap into your intuition

I was driving to an event a few years ago and listening to Elizabeth Gilbert's book *Big Magic*. If you haven't read or listened to that book, then you must. It's like an enchanted shot of unicorn crack for the soul. (FYI, unicorn crack is a legal high.)

In the book, Elizabeth talks about how fear stopped her writing her first book and how in the end she overcame it and became a best-selling author. As I was driving along, I felt some weird electricity start coursing through every part of my body. Every hair on my body stood up and it felt as if my blood was tingling. I had this almighty feeling, *knowledge*, that I should and would write a book. That's the incredible thing about your Soul: it can communicate with you in many different ways – through inspiration, ideas, or, my personal favourite, 'God bumps', more commonly known as goose bumps.

But guess what? … I ignored it for a while.

'Don't be so ridiculous – you are nobody!' whispered my Ego.

That was until one year later when I was asked to be honest, like really honest about what I wanted to do with my life and how I could make a bigger impact on the world. So, I wrote down in big fat letters 'WRITE A BOOK'. I just knew that this was something I had to do, and it was time to grow my lady-balls into big fat cahunas.

OK, so here is the deal: getting a book deal is notoriously hard, and, in my world, I was nobody. I was just a girl with a big dream. But I just knew it was what I wanted and what I could do. Where did that warm comforting blanket of 'knowing' come from? It came from my Soul. I was allowing it to shine. I trusted it like a mother and listened to it devoutly.

The series of events that unfolded after that was nothing short of miraculous. Once you start listening to the nudges of your Soul, you will start to see clues everywhere that you are being guided towards whatever your heart desires. Having admitted that writing and publishing a book was what I wanted, and while crafting my plan for doing this, I had full faith that it would happen – because your Soul never lies to you. In moments of doubt or in the face of rejection, I would ask the Universe for a sign and the sign would always appear – this is how I had the confidence that it would manifest, and, despite the odds being against me, I got offered a deal by two publishers.

When I looked back over that year and how I got here, all I can do is grin like the Cheshire Cat. It all made sense: each rejection had an important role in guiding me to the book deal that I knew would allow me to do big things in this world and to reach people with a message that in my heart is so important – that we all have the ability to change our lives if we choose to and that one important part of this is learning to choose whom we want to be, reprogram our minds and listen to our higher selves – our Souls.

OK, so how did I get to a point where I quietened down the Ego to make way for my intuition so I could learn to trust it. It's almost so simple that you will hate me. But yet so many people won't do it.

Quieten the noise

Meditation helps quieten the noise of the Ego. You really have an incredible opportunity to cultivate your intuition with solitude and silence, even for five minutes a day. This quiet time allows your mind a chance to spring-clean to give space for your Soul to communicate with you.

If you've never intentionally practised being alone, this can be a bit jarring. When you're alone, you are faced with yourself – all parts of yourself – in a raw way. Sometimes there can be emotions that surge unexpectedly from your inner core. Don't worry – this is part of the process of understanding yourself, allowing you to better recognize your intuition.

The best thing about being alone is you don't have other people around to tell what you should do or who you should be. You're left with yourself and your own decision-making power. And while it takes patience and practice to allow your mind to quieten, it's also incredibly freeing.

I have created a meditation exercise for tapping into your intuition and you can access it at www.noorhibbert.com/book.

Dance in ecstasy

Our most natural state is that of joy and love. When you are in this state, you are most connected to your intuition and have a heightened ability to *feel* it is communicating with you. Most of us ridiculous humans are totally oblivious to this 'natural state' because we are too busy feeling sorry for ourselves – maybe because it's a little rainy outside or the traffic is bad or our boss is being a douchebag. We get so caught up in the bullshit instead of absorbing the pure excellence that life truly has to offer.

If we took the time to appreciate what is in front of us, we would be going through shouting 'Amen!' from the rooftops. This feeling of total gratitude is our natural state. In fact, it's unbelievably easy to tap into our natural state yet, because it's that simple, we – complex humans that we are – just don't trust it.

Learning to trust

The thing about intuition is that our mind and our Ego will, most of the time, try to override it. They will attempt to talk us out of listening to it. Logical reasoning, practicalities and realism will kick in and will shut down what appears to be the 'mystical' guidance provided by your Soul.

Learning to trust it is *hard*. It's like that game where you have to fall backwards and hope that the person behind you hasn't forgotten to catch you. Sometimes your gut wants you to invest in something that feels impossible or go somewhere that feels out of reach or do something that quite honestly scares the living crap out of you. But, once you start seeing things happen, you develop confidence and trust in your intuition amid the chaos of your overly conditioned mind.

Let's say you are on the hunt for Mr Right/Ms Right. You end up dating someone who on paper ticks all the boxes. They are funny, attractive and kind and seems to have a nice mother-in-law who won't drive you bonkers should you decide to go the long haul. These are all things which are good on paper, but there's something inside of you that says this isn't the right fit. That's your intuition. You may end up staying with that person for a year (there's nothing wrong with that), but during the process it can be helpful to record your intuitive experience in a journal, what you did with it, and where it led you.

If they turn out to be a serial killer, or develops a disturbing penchant for licking your toes, just note it down and thank your intuition for letting you know in advance (despite the fact you ignored it for a while). This way you will know for the next time and save a year of your life in the long run. I had a friend who would always meet these men who seemed amazing and yet strangely she always felt 'red flags' popping up inside. That didn't stop her from taking the bait, however, and she endured years of heartbreak as a result.

Take action based on your intuition

Eventually, you will want to act on your intuition – unlike my dear friend who endured a decade of Mr Wrongs. You already do this on a subconscious level with small things (you eat when you're hungry and sleep when you're tired), but with bigger gut feelings it can take a little faith to step out there and act on a hunch.

Start small. If you're at a new restaurant and scanning the menu, choose the first item that sounds delicious. If you're running around the park and feel like you can do one more lap, then do it! This is training your mind, body and spirit to trust what naturally arises. As you become more comfortable with trusting your gut, you can begin using your intuition to inform bigger decisions such as:

- changing careers
- starting or growing your family
- investing in a course or mentor
- saying goodbye to toxic relationships, or
- mending broken ones …

But be aware that, despite acting on your gut, fear will still rear its scary face. Fear is always present when you do something big and new, but when it comes and tries to stop you doing something big, step back, witness it and verbally make a declaration that you choose not to listen to it.

Intuition and dharma (your purpose)

The easiest path to your purpose is to follow what lights you up. Think about what makes you feel excited, alive, awake. Books? Food? Travel? Helping people? Creating art? Wherever your joy is, that's where your purpose lies. Find those things that fill you with joy and your purpose will find you! Your Soul speaks in your emotions, so listen to them.

Don't be scared to turn inward and ask your intuition: What is my purpose? How can I help the world? How can I serve? Your inner wisdom (Soul) will provide you with guidance; you just have to listen and be on the lookout. Once you ask and stay tuned in to UniverseFM, you will start to see clues, but you just trust your gut. The Universe will start to pull you forward in the right direction with creativity or ideas that I call 'divine downloads'. It's literally like downloading the right information you need straight from the Universe. These ideas will lead you to where you need to go or will help you uncover what your unique talents and skills are, and how you can use them to serve. Sometimes our unique talents won't make us the richest money-wise, but they can make us feel the happiest and most fulfilled.

You also need to be happy to let go of who you used to be in order to become what you might be. The more your life is cluttered with things, people and events that no longer serve you, the more you don't have room to let the Universe show up with the things that actually serve your true purpose. If you are so busy living a life that doesn't light you up, taking time off to just let go of those routines is essential. Each day make a conscious choice to let go of something unessential, so that your life will open up to receive, recharge and become more aligned with your true purpose. That's why quietening the noise and practising meditation are essential.

Making 'white space' in your day is another important factor and something we all struggle with. Doing 'nothing' is nourishment for our Soul (note: binge-watching Netflix doesn't count as nothing!). The quality of your 'nothing' matters. And being out in nature is one of the best ways to slowly build these pockets of 'nothing' into your every day, to invite more 'being' into your life. This will provide you with the powerful opportunity to align yourself with the cycles of nature and the energy of the Universe and allow you to connect with your own being. After all, we are called human beings, not human doings.

Spiritual signage

If you doubt your intuition, then you can always ask for a sign from the Universe. Signs come in two forms: the ones you ask for and synchronicities. Synchronicities, or 'happy coincidences', occur when the Universe uses signs to show you that you are on the right path – the one aligned with your purpose. We are always guided through to our next step – we just need to follow those guiding lights to confirm we are heading the right way.

I want to share a story from when I gave birth to my third child. Let me start by saying that I know that when I need a sign it will deliver. For the past year, my sign has been a butterfly. If I need some reassurance on something, I'll ask and it will appear, but here's the caveat – the sign may not appear exactly how you imagined it.

I was walking around my kitchen at 37 weeks' pregnant and feeling my Braxton Hicks going into overdrive. I have always suffered from Braxton Hicks, so much so that, with my second child, my doctors were convinced that I was going into early labour, so I wasn't too alarmed. But there was this tiny voice inside of me saying, 'This is it – you're going into labour.'

I jokingly said to my husband that I had to know for sure as his parents were going to a wedding and I really needed them not to be inebriated in case they had to babysit. So, I stood in my kitchen and said out loud: 'Universe, do your thing. Show me a butterfly if I'm going into labour tonight.'

I then carried the salad I had made over to the table where my husband and children were eagerly awaiting their dinner. As I dished out the salad, a small piece of red onion (it looked purple) flew out of the bowl. I went to pick it up and put it back in when my three-year-old girl exclaimed, 'MUMMY, don't take my butterfly away!'

I had learned before that signs don't have to be that literal and I also knew that the Universe is a major show-off. The hairs on my arms stood up as my Soul communicated with me and I looked over at my husband. 'Holy shit!' I said, 'I think I'm going into labour!'

Five minutes after eating, I stood up, went to the living room and, as if perfectly orchestrated, I felt the pop as my waters broke in the middle of my living-room floor. 'Holy fuck! You really do have my back.'

That evening I welcomed my third daughter into the world in the exact birth I had manifested. I wanted a home birth. I wanted it to be at night so my children could sleep. I wanted my mother-in-law to be there. I wanted it to be calm and quick. I got it all. I asked for the sign and it showed up.

Sometimes signs come in other forms. They can come in certain numbers that keep showing up, or in animals that keep making an appearance (yep, there are such things as spirit animals!). If you keep your ears pricked and your eyes peeled, you will become aware that the Universe is always communicating with you.

TOP TAKEAWAYS
· ·

- Your intuition is the way the Universe speaks to your Soul.
- You need to quieten the Ego in order to listen to what the Soul is saying.
- You must practise trusting before you can trust.
- Make 'white space' in your day so you can connect with and drop back into your Soul.
- The Universe will always find a way of communicating with you, if you ask.

JFDI!

Document your divine downloads

Keep an intuition journal or write notes on your phone. Record similar intuitive feelings and experiences you have from day to day and week to week. Test your intuition out by asking questions and seeing what the different options feel like and what ideas come forth.

After a month or two, read back through your intuitive experiences and notice whether there are any patterns. You'll get to know yourself even more and understand how intuition appears in your daily life. There will always be distractions along the way, but your gut offers insights you won't find anywhere else, and it's worth nurturing.

11

Gratitude is So Dang Gangster

Gratitude is the quickest way to tune in to UniverseFM and makes way for healing to occur, for miracles to happen and for your desires to manifest.

We've done some serious work together and I hope that you feel awakened to a new sense of self and possibility. I would like you to take a moment to celebrate the fact you are right here, in this moment. I want you to be grateful that you have taken this opportunity to grow.

While thinking about my own personal development journey, I realized that it all stemmed from my mother. She joined a network marketing company and suddenly she was sticking goal planners on her wall, purchasing books by the dozen, walking around with an unusually sunny disposition and forever trying to sell us *Aloe vera* products. In all honesty, we thought she had joined a cult as she attended weekly meetings and kept trying to recruit unsuspecting members of the family to go with her. But she seemed really happy, and even though we thought she was being brainwashed, she kept talking about the Universe and energy. Something about it clearly attracted me on a subconscious level.

Once, at the end of a visit to my mother's home in Surrey, I grabbed a box set of Jim Rohn CDs (Rohn, 1994) that was sitting on her bookshelf next to an impressive range of self-development literature, so I had something to listen to on my three-hour drive back home to Yorkshire. This was the beginning of a new chapter: network marketing saved my life and the best part was that I never had to sell one *Aloe vera* product! An audiobook steered me towards an understanding that there is so much more to life than I had ever believed. And for that I am forever grateful.

Being grateful

Being grateful is something that we can all do but which costs us nothing, is simple to execute and takes little time. This chapter is going to give you the understanding of how gratitude is one of the most powerful ways to shift your energy and attract what you want into your life. Gratitude is the quickest way to tune in to UniverseFM and makes way for healing to occur, for miracles to happen and for your desires to manifest.

The truth is that we could all do with being more grateful. We are all so afflicted with the 'What's next?' syndrome that we forget to actually stop and be thankful for what we have in front of our eyes. It's actually one of the Ego's favourite games to play – the 'you haven't got what you want' game. In fact, the Ego convinces you that you need the car, the house, the promotion, the money *before* you can be happy or grateful.

Well, I'm here to shower all over the Ego's parade and tell you that, if you start becoming obsessively grateful for what you have right now, all those things that you desire will come to you a hundred times more effortlessly. The frequency of gratitude is the frequency of love, and the Universe is a hopeless romantic. Gratitude is so underused in our current world, in which we are more obsessed with moving forward instead of taking the time to enjoy where we are and what we have got right now.

So how can we become obsessively grateful each day? Well, go grab a piece of paper and make a list of all the ridiculously wonderful things you have. And I want you to dig deep. Forget about material possessions for now and think about what you *truly* have. If you are reading this book, then I'm going to take a guess that you are alive and can breathe. How often do you take a moment to be grateful that you can actually breathe?

Your first task here, then, is to take a deep breath in, one that truly fills every corner of your lungs. Do it right now. Now breathe out and say, 'I am grateful'. Do this daily.

If you are reading this book, then take a moment to be grateful for your eyes. If you are listening to this book, then be grateful for your ears. I would suggest that you lick the book to be grateful for your ability to taste, but I think that may be going too far!

The point is that we really have been gifted such incredible things – things that all too often we humans take for granted. How often do you take a moment to be grateful for the food on your plate, the clean water that you drink and shower with every day, or the people in your life? I have even started to become grateful for my bills. There are people in this world who would give their right arm for a water bill – a chance to not walk 15 miles to get a bucket of highly unsanitary water. When I shifted into a space of gratitude for being in a position where I could have those luxuries, my perspective dramatically shifted.

I don't want to go doom and gloom on you. I want you to start realizing the incredible abundance that you have right in front of you because, when you do, it will create more of what you want. The spiritual writer Eckhart Tolle talks about the need for us to be fully present in the moment and to appreciate every moment with sheer joy, for all we have is this very moment and what we have in this very moment is all we have right now.

Let's be real here: how often do you tell your partner, your kids, parents or friends that you are grateful for them? Engaging in unabashed appreciation can help nurture relationships like nothing else. It is quite shocking when I ask some of my clients when was the last time they shared their appreciation for their partners with their partners. Often the answer is 'I can't remember'. They may complain that their partners don't appreciate them or take them for granted yet have failed to notice that they do not act in the way they expect to be treated. Gratitude is a two-way street!

Practising gratitude

I always prescribe one month of gratitude giving. I tell my clients to write down a list of 30 things they are grateful for in their partners. The first ten will come easily; the middle ten will take a bit of time; the last ten will require some deep thinking. Write each one on a yellow stickie, and, every day for one month, leave a note for your partner somewhere they will notice: on a mirror, on their pillow, on their desk. Expect nothing in return. Watch the magic happening.

In addition to practising gratitude for all the good things you have, you must train yourself to also practise gratitude when life chokeslams you. Yes, you heard me – you need to become grateful not only when things go well but when things don't go quite so well. Because, when you are grateful, it's shifting your energy towards an understanding that 'This must be happening for the greater good'. When things feel hard or challenging or even devastating, keep repeating 'I'm grateful, I'm grateful, I'm grateful'. Fear and anxiety cannot coexist with appreciation.

Also, starting the day by announcing that you are thankful for having an absolutely amazing day will set you off on the right foot. I call this 'marinating your day'. In the same way I would marinate my food, I like to marinate my day. I like to soak my day in a special sauce of gratitude to ensure that it turns out exactly how I like. When you announce to the Universe how your day should work out, it paves the way for it to turn out just how you desire.

And add in the special words 'I am so grateful that today something incredible happened', and your vibe shifts from wanting something to stating that it's already here. If you look at the wording, you'll notice that it states your gratitude as though the good things *have already happened*. When you announce your gratitude in this way, there is a special power behind it that says, 'It's done'. Adapting the words of Stevie Wonder, 'Signed, sealed, delivered, it's yours.' The power is an energy force that speaks to the Universe. That energy is *faith*.

'Relax, mon'

Let's rewind to the autumn of 2007. I was walking up to this small shack on a beach in Jamaica, slightly pooping myself at the thought of going scuba diving. The man greeted me and my then-boyfriend and told us that he had space to take us out. The next minute we were ushered to this small boat that didn't even look safe enough to sit on the sand, let alone sail in water. I looked over at my boyfriend in total fear, wishing we had opted for drowning ourselves in rum daiquiris at the ever-so-safe swim-up bar.

What had I got myself into?

Before I knew it, we had boarded the boat alongside this Jamaican dude, who, I'm convinced to this day, was high as kite. It was he who was apparently going to teach us to dive. It hadn't occurred to me that we hadn't signed any safety paperwork and had had no training. The next minute we were in the middle of the ocean.

I have never ever been so terrified. The instructor, however, was super-relaxed. He kept saying 'Relax, mon' in his thick Jamaican accent as he did an unsettlingly swift demo of what we should do all the while attaching the scuba gear to my body. I couldn't relax, though. I was convinced that this was it. I would dive into the Caribbean Sea, never to return. I braced myself as he lowered a rope into the water and pointed for me to go down to the seabed.

'RELAX, MON.'

Our instructor must have said this a bazillion times and yet my heart was pounding so hard that trying to grasp this 'breathe through your nose' malarkey was proving almost impossible.

The good news is, of course, that I am here to tell the story. The bad news is that I did almost die as my tank nearly went down to zero because of my fast-paced, anxiety-induced breathing when I came face to face with a stingray. All I could see was my boyfriend using frantic arm movements to gesture to me to calm down while all I wanted to do was to punch him for suggesting this ridiculous expedition in the first place. Needless to say, I have never ever attempted to scuba dive since, and that relationship didn't last.

So, what do really scary, near-death scuba-diving experiences have to do with manifesting or success? Well, you need to learn to 'relax, mon', and have faith in the outcome. In order to acquire anything in the physical world, you have to relinquish your attachment to it. You need to fling your arms in the air and surrender to let the Universe do its thing. This doesn't mean you give up the intention of creating your desire. But you do give up your attachment to the result. Why? Because you know in every ounce of your Soul that the Universe will deliver.

So, while I may have desired to survive the scuba-diving experience, I was so attached to the outcome that I couldn't relax. The scuba-diving instructor, by contrast, was as cool as a cucumber, and I now realize that he must have been as spiritual as fuck.

It made me think how many times in my life I had been living in the future, wondering whether I would get the outcome I wanted. Would the boyfriend I had been dating for one week want to marry me? Would the business I had just started make me a million? Would I ever get abs from that new body treatment that promised to shrink me to a size 6 in ten minutes? The thing is, when we are always living in the future in a state of 'Why hasn't X or Y happened yet?', our energy around the subject becomes tainted. Where in *your* life are you so attached to the outcome?

Throw your hands up in the air, like you just don't care!

Surrendering to the Universe

One of the things that used to throw me off in the concept of 'surrendering to the Universe' is its relation to goal setting. The danger of falling into the 'Where is my ...?' trap is that every time you shift your thoughts into the *absence* of what you desire, it's like dropping a massive rock in front of the path of the Universe. It slows down the process of the manifestation. You may be wondering, as I once did, what is the point of having a desire if we then have to detach ourselves from it? Surely this is counterintuitive?

Well, an incredibly powerful thing happens when you throw your hands up in the air and act like you don't care ... it shows that you have faith. You still have the intention of reaching a goal, but you understand that, between where you are now and where you want to go, there is an infinite number of possibilities of how it could happen. The 'how' is not your business, baby – that is the Universe's job.

By combining intention with surrender at the same time, you will have that which you desire. What you are doing is factoring in the magic of uncertainty, which means that you are open to the journey changing on the spur of the moment if you find a better way to reach your goal. In addition, if you are open to the unknown occurring, you relinquish your need to force a solution and this keeps you open to the endless opportunities coming to you. I know this is mind-bending and can be confusing, but it all boils down to faith.

If you have unwavering faith that something bigger and way more powerful than you is here to support you, then you just *know* the outcome will be what you want. You don't need to constantly ask where it is or whether it will work. When we are attached to a result or outcome, this attachment has a foundation in my least favourite F-word – fear. This insecurity comes because faith is not present.

When you know that you have within yourself the ability to create whatever you want, you can then embrace the uncertainty of the journey with confidence. This will help you manifest more quickly, as this uncertainty allows for different options to flow. In order to make your dreams come true, you need to play the long game. If something is worth having, then it is worth having the patience it takes to get there.

I remember writing down that I wanted to do a TEDx Talk. I planned for it to happen in 18 months, during which time I would prepare by getting a few more low-key speaking gigs and doing film show reels and then approach TED later. My desire was there but I wasn't dwelling on it. Two weeks later, I received a call out of the blue asking me to do a TEDx Talk 48 hours later! I had nothing planned and it was scary as hell, but this is an incredible example of when things happen spontaneously because you're detached from the outcome.

As you can see, the Universe has the intelligence to orchestrate events to bring about the outcome that is intended. But when you are attached to that outcome, your intention gets locked into a rigid mindset and you lose the fluidity, the creativity and the spontaneity that are built into the Universe's field of possibilities.

The detachment also speeds up the manifestation process tenfold, as you can see from the TEDx example above. When you embody the notion of surrendering and have faith in it, you don't need to force solutions. Every time you catch yourself questioning where or why something hasn't happened for you, throw your hands into the air, wave them about and breathe it all out. Once you embrace uncertainty like a long-lost lover and adore it in the full knowledge that the result will manifest, what comes to fruition will utterly amaze you.

Uncertainty means stepping gracefully into the unknown in every moment of our life. At times, this can feel a bit like going on a brand-new roller-coaster. You climb into the seat, watch as the safety harness locks you in, and wait in anticipation for the speed of the ride. As the roller-coaster takes off, it's scary and gut-wrenching, and at times you wonder why on earth you opted for this crazy adrenaline rush, but you know there is an end to the ride. Then when you get off, you laugh at the questionable snapshot taken of you and it reminds you of all the fun that the ride brought you.

When you embrace uncertainty, you look for the excitement, fun, adventure and mystery of all the possibilities that may occur, even if that's scary. When you experience uncertainty, you are on the right path, so don't give it up. Although you have goals, and although you have mapped out a plan of how to reach them, you don't need to have a rigid idea of what you'll be doing next week or next year. Ultimately, this awareness that *anything* could unfold prepares you in the present moment – this is called preparedness.

Preparedness

When we focus on only the past or the future instead of the present, we prevent ourselves from being in the here and now. Being present is the only way we can reach consciousness and frees us from being locked into old behaviours.

This preparedness in the present moment means that you are more likely to seize an opportunity that may present itself to you. By practising the art of being prepared for uncertainty in any problem, you will be armed with the safe knowledge that there is an opportunity for something better to come out of it.

Think the 'Every cloud has a silver lining' type of thing. If your relationship is failing, choose to look at it as an opportunity to either fix it or to find someone else who is better suited to you. If you are up for redundancy, look at it as the opportunity you have been waiting for to start the business of your dreams or to get a new job with higher pay.

Once you adopt this mindset, you open up a whole range of possibilities and this keeps the mystery, the wonder, the excitement and the adventure alive, even when it feels like life is a hot mess. You can stay alert to opportunities by being grounded in the wisdom of uncertainty. When your preparedness meets opportunity, it is a cocktail for success because you have the trust that a solution will emerge that will bring a greater benefit to your life.

Some people call this good luck; I call it the Universe majorly having your back. Good luck is nothing but preparedness and opportunity shaking their tail feathers together.

TOP TAKEAWAYS

- Gratitude is something that we can all do that costs nothing and takes little time. Gratitude is the frequency of love.
- Practising gratitude allows you to practice appreciation for the present moment and what you have right now, rather than getting caught up in the 'what's next' syndrome.
- Marinate each day with gratitude and states it as though it has happened.
- Surrendering to the Universe and detaching from the outcome helps you to manifest your desires quicker.
- Don't be scared of the unknown. When you embrace uncertainty, you embrace the *adventure* of infinite possibilities.

JFDI!

Get grateful at gratitude

Keep a gratitude journal, and each day write five things that you are grateful for. Make this a daily ritual that gives you the space to tap into the present moment. Try to think of unobvious things that allow you to take your gratitude to a deeper level.

Make it your goal to always be on the lookout for blessings, as this will change your life and increase your happiness.

12

The Power of Your Posse

Stop taking constructive criticism from people who haven't constructed anything.

Let's talk about people. I've come to realize that no matter how much of an introvert or extrovert or any other type of 'vert' you are, we humans crave connection with other humans. But who we choose to spend our precious time with is of utmost importance.

Fitting in

Maslow's hierarchy of needs is a motivational theory in psychology made up of a five-tier model of human needs, often shown as levels within a pyramid. Needs that are lower down in the pyramid have to be met before dealing with the needs higher up. Starting from the bottom, the needs are physiological, safety, love and belonging, esteem and, at the top, self-actualization. Self-actualization is the full realization of one's creative, intellectual or social potential, or what I define as the understanding you have of your capacity to be more and do more. In essence, you realize that it's time to do your 'something big'.

Every person is capable and has the desire to move up the hierarchy towards the level of self-actualization. Unfortunately, sometimes the journey is disrupted by a failure to meet lower-level needs. So, in lame terms, if you don't have food or shelter, it will be very hard to go out and do your 'something big' in the world.

Right now, though, I want to talk about the third need, which is the social need to be loved and to belong. In order to avoid problems such as depression and anxiety, it is important for people to feel loved and accepted by other people. But what we need to be aware of is whether we are meeting this need in a way that will also help us achieve success. Are you choosing the right group of people to belong to that will help you reach your full potential?

I'll always remember a four-year period during my teenage years when I was trying to find my identity and where I would fit in. I think the defining moment for me was when I decided that I should be a Goth because that's what my friends were doing. We would traipse around Camden Market in London picking up studded dog-collar chokers, baggy Nirvana hoodies and black eyeliner. The 'Goth' phase came after the 'bright-pink pedal pusher trousers with really huge hooped earrings' phase. The truth is, I would have worn bin bags if that's what everyone else was doing.

I had a huge fear of standing out, being different or not feeling accepted. I also totally accept that, as we go through our teenage years, this is a time of exploration and that is totally OK. But, for me, it was more about conformity and a longing to be part of the group. This escalated as I grew older, so that I graduated from wearing clothes that matched other people's to doing drugs that matched other people's. Research has shown time after time the very great effect of our peers on our lives. If we aren't careful, the need to belong can take us down some very dark alleys.

Before becoming an entrepreneur, I worked in a sales job. Each day I would spend hours commuting between clients' houses and, after developing an aversion to listening to the same old songs on the radio, I dipped my toe into the world of audiobooks.

I became shamelessly obsessed with the American entrepreneur and motivational speaker Jim Rohn. I would spend hours just listening to him while in the comfort of my car. I'd never have guessed that spending so much time with a dead person would have brought me so much fulfilment. It was one of the first times that I really started to believe that I had the power to change my life. One of the things that stuck in my head is the notion that we are the sum of the five people we spend the most time with. We are all just balls of energy connected to one another so it makes total sense that the energy of those closest to us (not necessarily spatially) can have a profound impact and influence on how we feel and how we go about our own lives. For example, if you are around people who cheat on their partners and think it's OK, chances are that you will be influenced by them and do the same. If you spend your time with people who go out drinking every weekend, then chances are you will, too. Being in the wrong posse can have subtle yet long-lasting effects on your happiness and success.

Because it's human nature to want to fit in and be accepted, we all subconsciously conform to what feels like the safe option. We do this to feel that belongingness, even if those around us are behaving in ways that are not conducive to our success. While we all have the ability to think for ourselves, of course, we may unconsciously play along with the system and rules of those around us.

THE LITTLE SWALLOW'S STORY

I once read a story about a little swallow who was covering one of its eyes with its wing. An owl flew past and asked the swallow what was wrong. The swallow moved its wing and revealed a wound where its eye had once been. The owl nodded and said, 'Oh, I understand, you are crying because a crow pecked out your eye!' 'No,' said the swallow, 'I am crying because I let it.' This short yet profound fable illustrates the importance that we must become aware of the effect that those closest to us have on our mental, emotional and spiritual state.

Yes, we need to be loved and to belong, but it's equally important to make sure that the people around you have a positive effect on you and are not pecking away at your vision, like the crow did to the little swallow. Those who reach us on a daily basis should inspire us to be a better version of ourselves and should support us by accepting us when we show up as our most authentic self. The truth is that you could subconsciously be keeping yourself small and plodding along so that you don't get disowned by those you are closest to. The big question is: are you letting others steal your dreams?

Picking a new posse

Ask yourself: are the people around you going to support your journey? Do the people around you spend more time moaning and gossiping or motivating and inspiring? Do the people around you bring out the best in you? Every person gives off a vibe that will either energize you or drain you. Have you ever been around someone and said 'Oh, I get a negative vibe from them?' or 'She is so high vibe'? These are the exactly the vibrations I am talking about.

We literally emanate our vibes, and others can feel them and so can the Universe. You can't change how people want to go about their own life, but you can limit the effect they have on you if it isn't positive. I'd like you to empower yourself by knowing you can pick a new posse. Jim Rohn was the first person I picked in my posse. Yes, dead people also count. On a daily basis, I would spend more hours listening to him, letting him inspire me over and above the moans and groans of work colleagues and the dramas of my acquaintances. If you can't find a physical posse, then invest in buying a new posse through audiobooks or meeting people online to grow your network.

As you grow and develop, you may start to recognize that some people around you seem different. As you change, people around you may also change. Sometimes in a positive way and sometimes in a not so positive way. As you take the journey into becoming the best version of yourself, you will start to beam inside, and your light will shine bright. As much as it can inspire people, it can also reveal other people's imperfections. If people around you are supportive of you and this new chapter in your life, then that's marvellous and it may inspire them to make their own changes. If people begin to ignore you and start to pull away, then that's their loss. And God forbid that people dislike what you are doing or try to stop you – in that case, take a deep breath and stubbornly continue on your journey. Ultimately, you should never turn down the volume of your ambition because other people don't like the noise.

There is also a power in letting people go who bring too much drama into your life, even if you care about them. This can often be the hardest choice you will make. I was in a relationship with someone I truly loved but who brought out the worst in me. It wasn't his fault, but I always felt a level of tension as I tried to conform to the personality he expected his girlfriend to be. My intuition would consistently tell me that he wasn't right for me, but my Ego would always tell me there would be no one else better. I would go from being totally happy with him to falling into states of terrible anxiety, from having the best time to engaging in huge alcohol-fuelled arguments. My Soul was in constant conflict with my Ego, and this was causing inner turmoil.

If fear is keeping you in a relationship, it's time to exercise some huge self-love. Your romantic partner plays such a huge part in your life and is such an important member of your posse that you need to pick them very wisely. They will have the biggest impact on you and your success.

In addition, choose wisely who you share your dreams with. Have you ever told someone about your big plans and their initial reaction is to shoot you down or immediately tell you all the risks? If those people are not doing their own personal development work, then they will subconsciously project all their fears on to you because, when you go out and do immense things with your life, it will make them look and feel worse.

It's also crucially important that, as you venture into doing something new, you choose carefully who you take advice from. I cannot stress this enough. Often we seek advice from people who are not qualified to give us an answer, which puts us at a huge disadvantage.

Cara had desperately wanted to start a business for years, to give her freedom and to escape the 9–5. But every time she went to invest in a business coach, her husband would tell her, 'Oh, you can do it alone and save the money. Coaches are a waste of money.' Because Cara didn't know what she was doing, she always gave up. The irony here lay in the fact that Cara's husband wasn't an entrepreneur and had never invested in himself or a coach. But Cara loved her husband and his opinion mattered to her. Cara's husband wasn't doing this to be malicious and was ultimately trying to protect his wife from making a mistake. The intention was good, but it suffocated her dreams.

In fact, it's those who love us the most that usually are the most 'harmful' to our dreams. Their often-misguided advice comes from a place of protection which is fuelled by our old friend fear.

Cara put off her dream for many years until she finally decided to just fucking do it. And guess what? Cara is now the proud owner of a very successful six-figure business. The cost of bad advice can cause your Soul to go bankrupt. Had Cara never taken the leap, she would still be living a life that lacked fulfilment and freedom.

The lesson here is, whatever your goal is, you need to find people who have already done that 'something big'. Find the evidence from people who have got what you want and use them as your compass and inspiration. Fill your posse with inspirational folks.

Shortcut to success

I didn't want an easy life, I didn't want a comfortable life, I wanted an amazing life. So, I would go and find out from the people who inspired me how they created their lives. I read about millionaires, took courses with experts and invested in upgrading my mindset. I looked at the habits of successful people and I started to copy what they did. This is how you make sure that your new identity is conducive to success.

When I first started my physical products business, I didn't Google to just try to get information, I went straight to the people who were turning over millions a month on their businesses online and I learned from them. When I started my coaching business, I wanted to learn from coaches who were reaching the income goals I desired and making an impact on the world, in the way that I wanted to make an impact on the world. I went and invested in learning with them because mentorship is the shortcut to success.

If you want to lose weight and improve your health, get a personal trainer. If you want to be a great public speaker, invest in public speaking lessons. If you want a new business, invest in a business coach who has built that particular business well. I can guarantee there is someone doing the thing you want to do, and all you need to do is to find them. When you find someone who has achieved what you want, you can be sure that it can be done. You just need to take the same actions. Stop taking constructive criticism from people who haven't constructed anything. Don't take advice or listen to people who aren't doing what you want to do. Go straight to the source.

We're all human beings. Sometimes we put people we admire on a pedestal, and we think that they're superhuman. If there's someone who inspires you, reach out to them, and ask them the questions you want to ask. Say, 'Look, you've really inspired me. I would love to work with you. How can I get a chance for you to mentor me or work with me?'

Don't be scared to invest in something you really, really want. This is the secret of every successful person I've ever met.

Inspire, don't instruct

If you are wise enough to implement what I teach in this book, you will start seeing changes, and it's inevitable that you will want those around you to start doing the same. You may find yourself telling other people – perhaps your partner, or parents or friends – what to do. But fight that urge because inspiring others is a hundred times more powerful than *instructing* people.

I have clients forever telling me that their partners don't understand what self-development is and they find it frustrating that their partners won't meditate with them, do affirmations or write goals. The cold-hard truth is that people will only change if they *want* to. They can change only if they are ready. Don't get all evangelical with them, or you will be turning into a preaching mosquito, and mosquitos are an annoyance. Stay in your own lane.

JOANNA'S STORY

Joanna embarked on this journey of just fucking doing it in life. She started her own business and began to make more money, take lovely holidays, her relationships improved, and people started to take notice of her. However, there were a few people in Joanna's life who detached from her, and most of these were friends who were still in their old jobs, unhappy with their lack of fulfilment.

Instead of inspiring them, her success showed up their lack of desire to change their own lives and so they moved away from her.

We can't do anything about such situations. We need to accept and forgive these people and hope that they come back to us in good time, with their own new lives. But know this: for every person who cannot stand the brightness in your life, you will attract someone who will celebrate and embrace you and cheer you along your journey. You will find that you attract incredible new people into your life effortlessly. Sometimes, sadly, that involves saying goodbye to others.

Happy, not right

As discussed earlier in the book your words have the power to affect your energy, so make it your mission to be aware of how you speak of others, too. When you talk negatively about others, you are putting out some bad mojo. When you become defensive, play the blame game, or refuse to accept the moment, your life meets resistance.

Whenever you are confronted by a difficult situation or person, remind yourself: 'This moment is as it should be.' Becoming the best version of your spiritual self means giving up the need to convince or persuade others of your point of view. It's the Ego's game to always want to be right. If you start to look around, you will notice that people around you spend far too much time defending their point of view and it's a whole waste of energy. I'd much rather be happy than right, and when we don't play along with the Ego's need to be right we tap into an enormous amount of energy that we can use to make our life better.

Remember how I talked about you being an energy generator in Chapter 7? Think about the times you have become preoccupied by somebody else's dramas or have replayed a conversation that didn't go the right way, have obsessed about money, a promotion, a message left by an ex or a horrible experience that happened a year ago. Well, every time you negatively obsess about someone at work and how they never do their job properly, or an ex-partner and how they broke your heart, you are throwing out one of your energy cords and allowing them to suck away your energy.

You are giving your power away because in that moment you are lowering your vibe and giving away the power to change your life. Remind yourself that you have total control over who and what you chuck your energy cords out to. Some will suck you dry and drain you, and some will fill you up a treat and generate even more energy.

Choose to spend time with people who *fill* you up, people who you can truly be yourself around. They are your posse. Choose people who make you laugh. Laughter generates energy. Remember to nurture your relationships because if relationships aren't nurtured they die, just like plants. Take the time to pick a posse that lifts you up and then make a commitment to show those people the gratitude you have for them.

TOP TAKEAWAYS

- Your need to fit in can override your greatness because it can cause you to stay around people who stunt your growth.
- Surround yourself with people who inspire you. They don't need to be alive or in your physical presence.
- As you grow in your life, you may outgrow the people around you, and that's OK.
- Don't instruct the people around you to change; inspire them by changing and shining your bright light.
- Save your energy for important things: being happy is more important than the Ego game of being right.

JFDI!

Cut those cords

If you ever find yourself being mentally or emotionally drained by someone in your life, then it's time to release their mental stranglehold and cut the energy cord. Sometimes it's easy to get rid of a person *physically* from our lives, but we still spend so much time thinking about them that it still drains us. Sometimes we can't get rid of people physically, because they are a close family member, but you still want to get rid of the de-energizing effect they have on you. This is what this chapter's task is all about: reclaiming your power over your own energy cords.

The first thing you need to do in this task is to think about the people in your life who drain you. You need to work on one person at any given time. The first way to recalibrate your energy is to forgive people for anything they may have done. When we choose to forgive instead of holding grudges, we release the stagnant energy from our body that is stopping the flow of magic.

Grab a journal and write a letter of forgiveness to them. Let go of any anger, hurt, resentment and bask in the knowledge that they have come into your life to teach *you* how to become a better person. They are your lesson.

Once you have forgiven them, head to www.noorhibbert. com/book and listen to the cutting cord meditation to help you detach from them, energetically.

13

Don't Just Say It, Slay It

Like a rocket launching or a sausage rolling you need to just go-go-go before you let fear talk you out of it.

One night, between one too many Proseccos, I had an epiphany. Everyone, I thought, has a desire to change their lives in some way yet most people spend most of their time waiting for that change to magically occur. One of the biggest excuses I hear on repeat is 'I'm waiting for the right time', which, translated, means 'I'm scared'.

This then made me think that when I get drunk I am not scared – in fact, most people tend to do what the heck they want to do when they're inebriated. My inhibitions are lowered, and most times, regrettably, I become Billy Big Balls. The next morning I suffer from more than just a hangover – I experience the fear. The 'Oh shit, what have I done?' type of fear. I think the crowning moment for me was when, at my wedding reception, I decided to hurl myself on to the floor and roll on my side like a sausage, in my wedding dress. This, I can tell you, didn't end well.

However ridiculously I may have acted, there is a lesson here. We all need to be a little drunk in life and go shamelessly sausage-rolling towards our dreams. Lots of people will talk the talk of the things they want to do but stop before the necessary uncomfortable work of making it happen occurs.

But how do we go about slaying our goals like a ruthless ninja? First, we collectively need to stop caring about being perfect and getting it oh so right. I wasn't considering how to do the perfect sausage roll without damaging my expensive dress. Instead, I just hurled myself on to the floor, got on to my side and started rolling. There was no plan B. I was hell-bent on seeing my wedding-day gymnastics through.

Having the ability to take action without overthinking is one of the ingredients to creating success in all areas of your life. Like a rocket launching or a sausage rolling you need to just go-go-go before you let fear talk you out of it. A rocket doesn't start taking off, only to then just stop and question whether it should *continue* taking off. It just takes off ... whatever the consequences. When an idea comes to you or a desire makes itself known, you need to take action and quickly. Because if you don't, your brain will start coming up with a gazillion reasons why you shouldn't.

Why? Because, as you should know by now, your brain is designed to keep you safe and comfortable.

Once you do take off, you gain that incredible feeling of momentum. And the momentum is generative – it creates *more* momentum. Newton's First Law of Motion states that objects at rest tend to stay at rest, while objects in motion tend to stay in motion. So, the key is to get moving regardless of how hard it can be at first. Gain traction and you will get the power of momentum working for you early on. Then all you need to do is to go with the flow.

Take action ... fast!

As you start to gain momentum and realize that you are the captain of your ship, steering at the helm, it can be scary. You will encounter situations that will challenge you. It's inevitable because challenges are what create growth.

When faced with a new situation, our brains act like Google. When a new situation arises, it's as though your brain types in the new activity and does a search for relevant information. And if it's a brand-new situation such as building a new business or starting a new relationship, our brain does not have any data for it. So your brain just sees risk, as it doesn't have relevant data to give you a clear direction. Your brain will communicate with your nervous system, which will start telling you to stay away by making you feel scared. Or it will pull up data from past experiences that bear no relevance to the current one, and this will subconsciously induce negative feelings.

It's like one of those really annoying 'You have a virus' messages that scarily take over our computer screens. Your extraordinary life depends on you acting before that danger message pops up on your mental screen. The truth is, with anything new, there is the unknown, but, as we have discussed before, stepping into the unknown and having faith that the Universe will have your back is what will take you closer to your desires.

In addition, if you leave it too long to take action, your feelings get entangled in the decision. Research by the Portuguese neuroscientist António Damásio has shown that 95 per cent of our decisions are ultimately decided by feelings, not facts. He says that as humans we feel first then act second, rather than the other way around. This explains why so many of us often don't act at all because we simply 'don't feel like it'. To counteract this, then, take action fast!

BEN'S STORY

Let's talk about Ben. Ben kept complaining that he could never make the decisions that would take his business forward. (FYI, making decisions – even if they don't turn out to be right – is one of the traits of all successful people.) Ben had a habit of saying that he just needed to perfect things and that now wasn't the right time. When I questioned him about exactly what he needed to get perfect, he admitted that in fact he had everything in place but was just worried he would do it 'the wrong way'. Immediately before he was about to do something that felt difficult, scary or uncertain, he would hesitate. Ben was a class A procrastinator.

The curse of the two Ps

Procrastination and perfectionism are the kisses of death, people. They have nothing to do with ability. Procrastination is a form of stress relief. If you suffer from procrastination, then you need to understand what stress you are avoiding. And for most people it's fear of the outcome. I explained to

Ben that every time he hesitated, it triggered the virus sign to flash on his mental screen which was designed to stop him. And boom, the snooze button on his plans got pressed again. His lack of action was a kind of self-protection – it was like some heavy suit of armour that kept him safe but which also dangerously slowed him down. When we procrastinate, it stops us failing, and let's face it, failing is just as scary as taking action.

KATIE'S STORY

Katie hated to get things wrong. When things didn't go her way, it tumbled her into a vortex of feeling not good enough. She dangerously labelled herself a perfectionist and would proudly state it as though it were a good thing. There is nothing wrong with wanting to maintain an excellent standard in all you do but, if anything was out of Katie's control, it manifested itself as anxiety. She was so afraid of uncertainty that she wanted a guarantee before she tried anything new. She wanted evidence that, before she took the dart and aimed for the board, she would hit the bull's-eye – *perfectly*. She detested the feeling of discomfort that failure gave her because of experiences when she was younger, so she avoided it like the plague.

Perfectionism is just fear in a pair of Jimmy Choos – it may look like a pretty badge of honour but, once you've invested in being a perfectionist, it can stop you in your tracks because, although it looks pretty, it hurts. We self-sabotage by not taking action and we wrap it up in pretty excuse paper that has 'I need to get it perfect' printed all over it. Imperfect action is far more powerful that no action at all.

The excuses you are making are no less true tomorrow, next week or six months from now. If you start before you are ready and relinquish the need to prepare before you act, then I promise that you are just one decision away from changing your life. You need to just fucking do it.

Ain't nothing exciting happening in your comfort zone

You need to embrace failure and not to be scared to be punched in the face with it every single day. You need to strengthen your failure muscles so that every time things don't work out exactly how you planned, you can fight back. When you are scared of failure, you are at your weakest. One punch from failure will knock you down if you don't become friends with it. But if you pick yourself up and get back in the ring, you get stronger and stronger and the sting of failure dissipates.

So, I implore you to go out and momentously fuck up every day, as this will be a testament to how hard you are trying to go for your dreams. Don't fear failure, fear being stuck in exactly the same place in five years' time. After getting into the ring with failure enough times, you will embrace it like a long-lost friend and the punching will stop, because once you become best friends with failure, you aren't fighting it all the time. As with any sport, you need to first start and then you need to keep going until you win. You see, nothing worth having is in your comfort zone.

I was once asked to do a pilot for a TV show. When I read the proposal, I have to admit I was a little bit sick in my mouth. I was required to go and knock on the doors of complete strangers at 8 a.m. on a Saturday and ask whether they would like to start a business while being filmed doing it. First, I have never ever been on a TV show; second, there's nothing like a bit of cold-calling while on camera to make you want to puke up; and third, I felt the reality of a big dream perhaps coming to fruition and that was nerve-racking. The pressure was definitely on.

So, what did I do? Well, first I asked myself: 'Why am I scared? What is the bullshit story that is holding me back from knocking on people's doors?' Confront the fear and rationalize it. I needed to override the noise of my brain that was sensing risk and inducing fear. There was definitely an element of 'Am I good enough?', too, and also the fear of people slamming doors in my face while hurling expletives at me. But when I thought of the rewards in comparison to the risks, I knew it was time to see everything through the eyes of the woman who had courage. I needed courage. I needed to feel the fear and do it anyway.

In my younger years I would drink for courage and the beer goggles would give me the balls to do what I wanted. Well, I said goodbye to the beer goggles in my thirties and instead invested in some new fear goggles. I watched a film once where a dad gives his kid a pair of sunglasses on his first day at a new school and tells him they will make him invisible so he has the confidence to go to school – that is what I mean by my 'fear goggles'. I also spent the morning engaging in some serious tapping (see Chapter 5) to reduce my anxiety and by 8 a.m. I was ready to conquer the world.

I went to the first door, took a deep breath in an attempt to counteract the pounding of my heart and … 3, 2, 1 … knock knock knock. Nobody in. Thank God, I thought. But I had done it: my fist had touched the door. I can confirm that, with every small act of courage, more courage follows, and by the end of the day I was proudly knocking on doors with enthusiasm and excitement and speaking to total strangers. I'm happy to report that, notwithstanding the large number of 60-year-old bare-chested men, I got no expletives at all. Hashtag winning.

Courage is powerful. It feeds on itself, grows bigger, then leaks into other areas of your life and takes you closer to your extraordinary dream. What is the one thing you have been scared of doing that you know will take you closer to your goals? Your extraordinary life depends on you permanently switching off the snooze button, taking off your Jimmy Choos and embracing all that life has to offer, no matter how scary it is. Remember, you can put those fear goggles on whenever you want, and if you start telling me you don't have any, well, then you can borrow mine.

Nature is easy like Sunday morning

If you think about how nature works, you will see that everything is easy and flowing. Trees don't try to grow, they just grow. Birds don't try to fly, they fly. Fish don't try to swim, they just swim. It's in their nature. And I'm here to drum it into you that it is human nature to make our dreams manifest into physical form, easily and effortlessly. I like to call this miracle making.

When you go out there and start slaying life and going for your goals, remember to have fun and to remind yourself that having what you want does not need to feel hard. In fact, it should be the total opposite; it should flow like nature. Success comes easily when we follow the path of least resistance. The path of least resistance does not mean staying comfortable or avoiding getting out of your comfort zone. It means listening to your Soul and taking the aligned action towards your dreams.

Making sure that there is fun involved in everything you do and that all your actions are motivated by love will also serve you well in your quest for the awesome life that feels easy. You will find that you can do less to achieve more. This doesn't mean being lazy but doing the things that light you up and energize you to get the results you want. As I told you earlier, the Universe is a hopeless romantic and nature is held together by the energy of love.

Remember, love is not the default mode of the Ego. Attention to the Ego consumes the greatest amount of energy and will drain you, which will stop you ever feeling that level of happiness you crave. When your internal reference point is the Ego, when you seek power and control over other people or seek approval from others, you expend energy in a wasteful way. But if you stay in the lane of joy and remain motivated by love, you create energy which can then be channelled to create anything that you want.

Make a commitment to following the path of no resistance by engaging in activities and thoughts that bring you joy. If your goal is to lose weight and you hate running, then this is the most resistant path to losing weight. Find something that allows you to tune in to the channel of joy, perhaps by joining a dance or trampolining class or going swimming, because this will help you get to your goals ten times more quickly.

If you are setting up a business, find your unique talents and find the things that come easily and naturally to you. Stay in your own lane. The path of joy is where your dreams will manifest spontaneously, without friction or effort. Drop your comparison hangover, become immune to criticism, embrace challenge and harness the power of love, so that you can use that energy to create whatever the hell you want! And, most importantly, be consciously aware if your thoughts are helping you or hindering you, and make the necessary adjustment in that moment.

TOP TAKEAWAYS

- Momentum will be your best friend so keep moving, even if you are taking only small steps.
- Challenges create growth: don't fear them because real growth happens outside of your comfort zone.
- Imperfect action is far better than no action at all.
- Embrace the idea of failing instead of fearing it and enjoy the journey, even when it's scary.
- Make a commitment to following the path of no resistance by engaging in thoughts and things that make you happy.

JFDI!

Grow your courage

In this final JFDI! task I want to encourage you to do something that makes you feel utterly uncomfortable.

I used to play this game called 'Dead Ants'. I wish I could say that it was a childhood game, but in fact I was in my twenties when this game was introduced to me. We would be out and about and if someone shouted, 'Dead Ants!', you all had to get on to the floor on your back and wave your arms and legs in the air. It caused a spectacle for sure and the first time you took part it made you squirm with embarrassment. But, once on the floor, you'd find yourself laughing with delight at the ridiculousness of it all, and you would stand up thinking 'That didn't kill me' and go on your merry way.

It's not particularly socially acceptable to lie down in the middle of a street acting like a dead insect, but every time I participated in an activity that pushed 'normal' social boundaries, my courage and confidence grew.

So, in this task, it's time to warm up your failure muscle and have the courage to do something that scares you. What have you been putting off? What can you do today that will move you one step closer to your dream? What can you do that is silly and ridiculous and embarrassing? Push your boundaries. Go out and lie on the floor like a dead ant if you have to. Get someone to take a picture and hashtag it JFDI!

What the heck – I'll do it, too! Yep, I'm right there with you.

But for goodness' sake, just fucking do something – your extraordinary life depends on it.

Epilogue: Namaste, Bitches

As we come to the end of our journey together, I want you to think about a big question ... WHY? Why should you just get on and do the tasks? Why should you step into your greatness and go for your goals with gusto? Well, I'm here to ask you, why *not*?

What have you got to lose? Why not be the you with the money you desire, the body you dream of, the relationship that lights you up? Why not now? What are you waiting for? Take action NOW.

Don't wait for tomorrow to implement the changes in your life. Don't wait until tomorrow to give up the sugar. Don't wait until tomorrow to finally start that business. Don't wait until tomorrow to take salsa classes in Brazil. Whatever it is that your heart yearns for, it is already yours for the taking if you tune in to the frequency of the Universe and move gracefully towards that which you want following a plan that you can put your focus on.

And remember this, nobody is an overnight success. In psychology, there is a concept called relative deprivation. This is where you have the perception that you are worse off than the other people you compare yourself to. Having this feeling can lead to the comparison hangover I talked about in Chapter 4. Most of us compare our today to someone else's 20 years of hard graft. We haven't seen the work or sacrifices they put in behind the scenes. Don't be scared to put the work in because, as clichéd as it sounds, success is not the last stop on the journey. Success is the person you become as a result of the journey you take. Who you become as a result of stepping up and unapologetically being the best version of you is where the magic lies.

As I explained earlier in this book, when you look at someone else and it triggers envy, use that positively. Use that envy as a kind reminder from the Universe that you desire something and that it is meant for you, too. But don't be misled into believing you can click your fingers for it, because most successful people I've spoken to have put in the heart hustle to make it happen. (Heart hustle is the work you must put in to follow your heart's desires.) Be willing to work for your dreams and accept that it's going to get uncomfortable doing it. But oh so bloody worth it.

Let the power of your mind and the power of the Universe create your ideal life. Trust that you have all you need inside your incredible imagination to forge a life beyond your wildest expectations. Make a commitment to move past your limiting beliefs, ninja-kick your way through your fears and put yourself in the driver's seat. Stop giving a fuck about the little things in life that simply don't matter. Save your fucks for magical shit. Success is your absolute birth right. Remember to lead life through the lens of love and this will truly leave you Soul-ar-powered and tuned firmly in to UniverseFM. And if someone says you can't do what you want, do it twice and take a selfie.

Our time together and your journey of spiritual awesomeness and psychological transformation do not stop here. I have created some life-changing tools to help you stay focused and keep you motivated to become the best version of you – find them at www.noorhibbert.com/book.

Life really is the ticket to the greatest show on earth – are you ready to come join me in the front row?

Noor

Further Reading

Brand, Russell, *Recovery: Freedom from Our Addictions* (Bluebird, 2018)

Dyer, Wayne W., *The Power of Intention: Change the Way You Look at Things and the Things You Look at Will Change: Learning to Co-create Your World Your Way* (Hay House, 2004)

Gilbert, Elizabeth, *Big Magic: Creative Living Beyond Fear* (Bloomsbury, 2014)

Grout, Pam, *E-Squared* (Hay House, 2013)

Hill, Napoleon, *Think and Grow Rich*, revised edition (Mindpower Press, 2015)

Ravikant, Kamal, *Love Yourself Like Your Life Depends on It* (ebook, 2012)

Rinpoche, Sogyal, *The Tibetan Book of Living and Dying* (Rider, 2008)

Rohn, Jim, *The Art of Exceptional Living* (audiobook, Nightingale Conant, 1994)

Rohn, Jim, *7 Strategies for Wealth and Happiness*, (Prima Life, 1996)

Just F*cking Write It Down